KU-630-801

A
TASTE
OF
FAME

200 Celebrities Present their own Favourite Recipes

A
TASTE
OF
FAME

200 Celebrities Present their own Favourite Recipes

Compiled by David Scott

Futura

For my wife, Isobel,
and in memory of my late father
John Ray Scott

A Futura Book

© Futura Publications, 1986

First published in Great Britain in 1986 by
Futura Publications, a Division of
Macdonald & Co (Publishers) Ltd
London & Sydney

All rights reserved
No part of this publication may be reproduced,
stored in a retrieval system, or transmitted, in any
form or by any means without the prior
permission in writing of the publisher, nor be
otherwise circulated in any form of binding or
cover other than that in which it is published and
without a similar condition including this
condition being imposed on the subsequent
purchaser.

ISBN 0 7088 3183 4

Futura Publications
A Division of
Macdonald & Co (Publishers) Ltd
Greater London House
Hampstead Road
London NW1 7QX

A BPCC plc Company

Designed and edited by The Festival Press Limited,
5 Botts Mews, London W2 5AG
Recipes edited by Norma MacMillan
Illustrations by Michael McGuinness

KEY
✗ indicates recipes taking up to 30 minutes to prepare.
✗✗ indicates recipes taking between 30 minutes and
1½ hours to prepare.
✗✗✗ indicates recipes taking over 1½ hours to prepare.

Acknowledgments

The publishers would like to thank the many famous people who
have given recipes for use in this project, some of which could not be
used because of lack of space. The recipes have all been edited to one
consistent style but otherwise appear as the contributors donated
them.

The publishers have obtained permission to print wherever this was
in doubt. If any acknowledgments are omitted, the publisher should
be informed so that this error may be corrected for future editions.

Printed in Great Britain by
Hazell Watson & Viney Limited,
Member of the BPCC Group,
Aylesbury, Bucks

CONTENTS

FOREWORD

Like myself, you have probably experienced the loss of a relative or close friend through death caused by cancer, a disease which kills one in five of the population. Through research exciting discoveries promise great hope for the future as scientists begin to understand the disease. By applying knowledge already gained through research, doctors are able to treat, relieve and cure some patients who in the past had no chance of survival.

By purchasing this book you are helping to fund research into the causes and treatment of cancer, through the North of England Cancer Research Campaign. This organisation is affiliated to the National Cancer Research Campaign with whom it shares its research findings.

At present only a limited number of research projects can be allocated funds, so there is no room for complacency when it comes to raising money. With your help, and the help of all those who have so generously donated recipes for this book, the goal of conquering cancer could be brought much nearer.

David Scott

DAVID SCOTT

HALL OF FAME

A ★ **Russ Abbot** *comedian* escargots bourguignonne 29 ★ **Jean Alexander** *TV presenter* roast ham 71 ★ **Terence Alexander** *actor* bab ganouge 26 ★ **John Arlott, OBE** *cricket commentator and wine expert* cassoulet 84 ★ **Jane Asher** *actress* pasta, cheese and corn casserole 94 ★ **Michael Aspel** *broadcaster/writer* fillets of sole Meurat 42 ★ **Pam Ayres** *TV personality* Cotswold fandango 56

B ★ **Robin Bailey** *actor* moules marinières 29 ★ **Colin Baker** *TV journalist/presenter* Jansson's temptation 38 ★ **Richard Baker** *newsreader/presenter* fish crumble 38 ★ **Christiaan Barnard** *surgeon* veal scaloppine with tomatoes 64 ★ **Derek Batey** *compère/presenter* beef sauté chasseur 51 ★ **Alan Beith** *MP* orange pudding 113 ★ **Tony Benn** *MP* cup of tea 133 ★ **Allison Bettles** *actress* brandy snaps 138 ★ **Christopher Biggins** *TV presenter* Vichyssoise 22 ★ **Cilla Black** *singer* special prawn cocktail 32 ★ **Baron Stuart Blanch** *former Archbishop of York* frozen strawberry mousse 117 ★ **Peter Bowles** *actor* cheese and tomato toasty 109 ★ **Katie Boyle** *TV personality* chocolate pots 123 ★ **Willy Brandt** *former West German Chancellor* chicken in red wine 83 ★ **Richard Briers** *actor* caramel and apple soufflé 115 ★ **Rt Hon Leon Brittan** *MP* breast of chicken coriander 76 ★ **Duggie Brown** *actor/comedian* honey-glazed lamb 60 ★ **Basil Brush** *fox puppet* saltimbocca alla Romana 64

C ★ **Marti Caine** *comedienne/singer* sole with prawns 44 ★ **Tommy Cannon** *comedian* beef curry 55 ★ **Willie Carson** *jockey* roast grouse with brandy cream 83 ★ **Jimmy Carter** *former US President* 'plains special' cheese ring 108 ★ **Barbara Cartland** *author* chicken with orange surprise 82 ★ **Roy Castle** *entertainer* chocolate party gâteau 125 ★ **Jack Charlton OBE** *former England footballer* banana cake 136 ★ **John Cleese** *actor/writer* mock ferret soup 13 ★ **Brian Clough** *football club manager* family turkey pie 85 ★ **Sebastian Coe** *athlete* spaghetti vitello 63 ★ **George Cole** *actor* stuffed peppers 106 ★ **Billy Connolly** *comedian* stuffed trout 41 ★ **Catherine Cookson** *author* American bite 109 ★ **Henry Cooper** *boxer* steak and kidney pie 52 ★ **Jilly Cooper** *author/journalist* baked tomatoes 96 ★ **Ronnie Corbett OBE** *actor/comedian* baked apple and almond pudding 114 ★ **Robin Cousins** *skater* carrot cake 137 ★ **Frances Coverdale** *newsreader* lemon syllabub 112 ★ **Michael Crawford** *actor* chicken and leek pie 79 ★ **Bernard Cribbins** *actor* spicy prawns 33

D ★ **Billy Dainty** *comedian* watercress soup 21 ★ **Paul Daniels** *magician* liver pâté 35 ★ **John Dankworth CBE** *musician* gazpacho 24 ★ **Windsor Davies** *actor* lava bread 103 ★ **Peter Davison** *actor* hamsteak Hawaii 70 ★ **Les Dawson** *comedian* risotto 102 ★ **Christopher Dean MBE** *skater* Weinacht's cream 120 ★ **Judi Dench OBE** *actress* smoked mackerel pâté 34 ★ **Barbara Dickson** *singer* vegetable tarts *99* ★**Ken Dodd OBE** *comedian* steak Diane *50* ★**Betty Driver** *actress* salmon kedgeree *39*

E ★**Paul Eddington** *actor* Jerusalem artichoke soup *15* ★**Don Estelle** *actor* shrimp potato balls *39* ★**Sir Geraint Evans** *singer* trout with almonds *41* ★**Dame Edna Everage** *entertainer* Aussie lamingtons *139*

F ★**Douglas Fairbanks Jr** *actor* Hungarian yogurt soup *23* ★**Michael Fish** *TV weatherman* pasta carbonara *92* ★**Rt Hon Michael Foot** *MP* parsnip and orange soup *16* ★**Marian Foster** *journalist/broadcaster* strawberry cardinal *117* ★**Trevor Francis** *footballer* steak Argentine *49* ★**Fiona Fullerton** *actress* pâté-stuffed chicken breasts in Marsala cream *76*

G ★**Billy Graham** *evangelist* fresh apple cake *142* ★**Leslie Grant** *actor* marinara *40* ★**Sir Ron Greenwood** *former England football manager* spaghetti with curried beef sauce *106*

H ★**Stuart Hall** *TV presenter* hazelnut rolls *134* ★**Judith Hann** *TV journalist/presenter* grilled breast of lamb *60* ★**John Hanson** *singer/actor* stuffed marrow [squash] *104* ★**Mike Harding** *comedian* Allensuppe *18* ★**Rolf Harris OBE** *entertainer* bachelor scrambled eggs and

tomatoes *132* ★**Tony Hart** *painter/TV presenter* roast duck in orange sauce *84* ★**Russell Harty** *TV journalist* savoury pork chops *66* ★**Nigel Hawthorne** *actor* chilled avocado soup *22* ★**Rt Hon Denis Healey MBE** *MP* rhubarb fool *122* ★**Rt Hon Edward Heath MBE** *MP* French onion soup *14* ★**Paul Heiney** *TV presenter* plum duff *128* ★**James Herriot** *author* panacalty *104* ★**Jimmy Hill** *sports presenter* curried chicken with peaches *75* ★**Vince Hill** *singer* oxtail casserole *58* ★**Diane Holland** *actress* pascha *126* ★**Fred Housego** *Mastermind champion* pollo cacciatora *80* ★**Rt Hon Sir Geoffrey Howe** *MP* hotpot *54* ★**Frankie Howerd OBE** *comedian* cold lemon soufflé *112* ★**Roy Hudd** *comedian* sausage and tomato pie *69* ★**Geoffrey Hughes** *actor* pork chops with sage and apple *67* ★**John Hurt** *actor* Donna's Texas chilli *57* ★**Olivia Hussey** *actress* sashimi *37*

I/J ★**Jeremy Irons** *actor* champ *87* ★**Glenda Jackson** *actress* cassata di mascaponi *127* ★**Gordon Jackson OBE** *actor* crumpets *134* ★**Derek Jacobi** *actor* cheese and potato pie *109* ★**David Jacobs** *TV compère* roast beef with Yorkshire pudding *48* ★**David Jessel** *TV journalist* Ben and Robert's rangapanga pie *116* ★**Stratford Johns** *actor* spinach, cheese and egg grill *88* ★**Peter Jones** *actor/author* apple and mincemeat crumble *115* ★**John Junor** *national newspaper editor* oatcakes *135*

K ✦ Gorden Kaye *actor* pears in tarragon cream 33 ✦ Penelope Keith *actress* gougère 88 ✦ Rt Hon Neil Kinnock *MP, Leader of UK Labour Party* roghan gosh 55 ✦ Anne Kirkbride *actress* layered chocolate soufflé 124 ✦ Jimmy Krankie *comedian* clootie dumpling 138

L ✦ Cleo Laine OBE *singer* veal in paprika sauce 65 ✦ Bob Langley *writer/broadcaster* rough-style pâté 34 ✦ Eddie Large *impressionist/comedian* steak à la Eddie 49 ✦ Sue Lawley *broadcaster/journalist* argentan 125 ✦ Syd Lawrence *band leader* queen of puddings 129 ✦ Jan Leeming *newsreader* mackerel mousse 28 ✦ Geoff Lewis *Lloyd's chef* velouté mignon 43 ✦ Lord Lichfield *photographer* Wiltshire leek soup 15 ✦ Robert Lindsay *actor* chicken stuffing 78 ✦ Desmond Lynam *journalist/broadcaster* macaroni cheese de luxe 95

M ✦ Don Maclean *comedian* crab quiche 40 ✦ Alfred Marks OBE *actor/comedian* stuffed mushrooms 26 ✦ Millicent Martin *actress/singer* smoked salmon dip 27 ✦ Clarissa Mason *widow of James Mason* gâteau gaffe 126 ✦ Paul McCartney *song writer/singer* green pea soup 20 ✦ Ian McCaskill *TV weatherman* spaghetti sauce 107 ✦ Paul McDowell *actor* avocado mousse 25 ✦ Yehudi Menuhin *violinist* stuffed aubergines [eggplants] 98 ✦ Lord Miles CBE *theatre manager* bacon roll pudding 103 ✦ Sir John Mills *actor/producer/director* mango and prawn cocktail 33 ✦ Maj-Gen Sir Jeremy Moore *Commander Land Forces, Falkland Islands 1982* gooseberry tart 119 ✦ Patrick Moore OBE *astronomer* curry

à la Selsey 74 ✦ Brian Murphy *actor* bangers and mash 70

N ✦ Derek Nimmo *actor* iced curry cream soup 23 ✦ Trevor Nunn *director* chicken fillets in herb mustard sauce 77

O ✦ Ian Ogilvy *actor* turnip and onion soup 17 ✦ Bill Owen *actor* chicken paprika 76 ✦ Rt Hon David Owen *MP, Leader UK SDP* kidneys in butter and mustard sauce 62

P ✦ Nicholas Parsons *actor/compère* melon and tomato cocktail 33 ✦ Jon Pertwee *actor/comedian* thick spinach soup 21 ✦ Leslie Phillips *actor/director* avo dip 25 ✦ Pat Phoenix *actress* egg and tuna pickups 91 ✦ Ron Pickering *commentator* barbecued spareribs 68 ✦ Lester Piggott OBE *jockey* cheese soufflé 90 ✦ Alan Plater *playwright* boiled eggs 131 ✦ Donald Pleasance *actor* sole bonne femme 44 ✦ Gwyneth Powell *actress* coronation chicken 78 ✦ Rt Hon James Prior *MP* banana ice cream 111 ✦ David Puttnam *director* ossobuco Milanese 66

Q/R ✦ Anthony Quayle CBE *actor* tripe Catalane 58 ✦ Esther Rantzen *TV journalist/presenter* consommé Pettifer 22 ✦ Claire Rayner *journalist* vegetable lasagne 92 ✦ Christopher Reeve *actor* spaghettini alla vongole 95 ✦ Cliff Richard *singer* Christmas tartlets 140 ✦ Wendy Richards *actress* bread and butter pudding 129 ✦ Diana Rigg *actress* gigot de mouton boulangère 61 ✦ Brian

Rix *actor/manager* tripe and onions *59*
★ **Robert Robinson** *TV and radio compère/ commentator* brandy bananas *111*
★ **Bobby Robson** *England football team manager* beef Wellington *47* ★ **Bryan Robson** *England footballer* sautéed king prawns *32* ★ **Jean Rogers** *actress* baked peaches with orange sauce *118* ★ **Ted Rogers** *comedian* cream of tomato soup *17*
★ **Nick Ross** *TV presenter* moch pudding *116* ★ **Most Rev and Rt Hon Dr Robert Runcie** *Archbishop of Canterbury* eggs with shrimps *90*

S ★ **Paul Scofield CBE** *actor* kidneys with mushrooms and yogurt *57* ★ **Selina Scott** *TV journalist/presenter* bacon and egg pie *102* ★ **Sir Harry Secombe CBE** *singer/ comedian* Welsh cakes *141* ★ **Rt Rev David Sheppard** *Bishop of Liverpool* traditional Lancashire hotpot *62* ★ **Valerie Singleton** *TV journalist/presenter* toffee-topped peaches and cream *118* ★ **Delia Smith** *cook* curried cream chicken *73*
★ **Mel Smith** *actor* blackcurrant sorbet *122*
★ **Diane Solomon** *singer* gingerbread *136*
★ **Rt Hon David Steel** *MP, Leader UK Liberal Party* Welsh rarebit *108* ★ **Pamela Stephenson** *comedienne* Pamela's pasta with vegetable surprises *93* ★ **Miriam Stoppard** *TV presenter/author* summer pudding *128* ★ **Una Stubbs** *actress/dancer* muesli *131*

T ★ **Jimmy Tarbuck** *comedian* vegetable soup *18* ★ **Rt Hon Norman Tebbit** *MP, Chairman UK Conservative Party* mussels in wine cream *45* ★ **Rt Hon Margaret Thatcher** *UK Prime Minister* cold chicken Veronique *81* ★ **Gareth Thomas** *actor* Welsh spareribs *69* ★ **Angela Thorne**

actress crème brûlée *127* ★ **Jayne Torvill MBE** *skater* Weinacht's cream *120* ★ **Dave Lee Travis** *disc jockey* beef stroganoff *53*
★ **Dorothy Tutin CBE** *actress* salmon mousse with cucumbered sour cream *27*

U/W ★ **Tracey Ullman** *comedienne/ actress* Polish snack *105* ★ **Julian Lloyd Webber** *cellist* lychee and orange compote *113* ★ **John Wells** *actor* nourishing million calorie breakfast *132*
★ **Geoffrey Wheeler** *TV presenter* mincemeat cakes *135* ★ **Lord Whitelaw** *MP* Cumberland sauce *71* ★ **Kenneth Williams** *actor/comedian* prune mould *120*
★ **Rt Hon Shirley Williams** *Chairman SDP* lemon pudding *112* ★ **Bob Wilson** *sports presenter* courgettes maison *97*
★ **Lord Harold Wilson** *MP, former UK Prime Minister* apple charlotte *114*
★ **Julian Wilson** *horse racing commentator* baked egg with sweetcorn *103* ★ **Norman Wisdom** *actor/comedian* stuffed baked potatoes *97* ★ **Ernie Wise OBE** *comedian* steak and vegetable casserole *54* ★ **Terry Wogan** *broadcaster/presenter* chip buttie *101* ★ **Victoria Wood** *comedienne/ writer* vegetable casserole *99* ★ **Barbara Woodhouse** *animal trainer* lemon cake *135*

Y ★ **Mike Yarwood** *impressionist* seafood au gratin *30* ★ **Susannah York** *actress* pasta cosa nostra *94*

SOUPS
AND
STARTERS

HOT SOUPS

JOHN CLEESE
●
MOCK FERRET SOUP

Ingredients
To serve

Metric/ Imperial		American
1	*ferret*	1

Method

Put the ferret in a large barrel from which it cannot escape. Then mock it with such phrases as 'Oh, what a silly old ferret you are', or 'Not only do you have a long nose but also your legs are somewhat bandy', or 'It is generally agreed that you could not chase a vole let alone a rabbit', or 'Even by ferret standards you are unimpressive'.

When the ferret is mocked, simmer in the Bay of Biscay, and serve with a writ for libel.

'What the press say about ferret recipes: ''I have never tasted food like it before.'' Observer ''I shall certainly tell all my friends.'' Guardian ''I shall certainly tell both my friends.'' The Listener Ferret recipes from David Frost at the Phonograph. Your chef John Cleese – meal in a moment.' JOHN CLEESE

EDWARD HEATH
•
FRENCH ONION SOUP

Ingredients
To serve 4 ✖✖

Metric/ Imperial		American
4	large onions	4
25 g/1 oz	butter	2 tbsp
1.2 l/2 pints	beef stock	5 cups
	salt and pepper	
4	slices of bread	4
100 g/4 oz	grated Cheddar cheese	1 cup

Method
Peel the onions and slice them thickly. Heat the butter in a heavy saucepan and fry the onions over moderate heat until soft and golden brown (not burnt). Stir from time to time to prevent sticking. Pour in the stock and bring to the boil. Cover and simmer for 30–45 minutes. Add seasoning to taste.

Just before the soup is ready, toast the slices of bread (first removing crusts if you are fussy).

Ladle the soup into individual bowls and float a slice of toast on each serving. Sprinkle generously with the grated cheese. This is a meal in itself.

PATRICK LICHFIELD
•
WILTSHIRE LEEK SOUP

Ingredients
To serve 4–6 ✗✗

Metric/ Imperial		American
225 g/8 oz	leeks	½ lb
4	bacon slices	4
50 g/2 oz	butter	¼ cup
1½ tbsp	flour	1 tbsp
900 ml/1½ pints	chicken stock	2 pints
2 tbsp	grated Parmesan cheese	2 tbsp
150 ml/¼ pint	single [light] cream	½ cup
4 tbsp	chopped fresh parsley	¼ cup
	salt and pepper	

Method
Wash the leeks thoroughly, then slice them thinly. Chop the bacon, first removing any rind. Heat the butter in a saucepan and cook the leeks and bacon until soft but not browned. Add the flour and stir well, then stir in the stock. Bring to the boil, stirring, and simmer until thickened.

Add the Parmesan cheese and stir until melted. Stir in the cream, parsley and seasoning to taste. Heat through and serve piping hot.

LICHFIELD

PAUL EDDINGTON
•
JERUSALEM ARTICHOKE SOUP

Ingredients
To serve 6 ✗✗

Metric/ Imperial		American
900 g/2 lb	Jerusalem artichokes	2 lb
	juice of ½ lemon	
1	small onion	1
50 g/2 oz	butter	¼ cup
	salt and pepper	
900 ml/1½ pints	chicken stock	2 pints
600 ml/1 pint	milk	2½ cups

Method
Peel the artichokes and cut them into small pieces. As they are prepared, drop them into a bowl of water that has had lemon juice added to it; this will keep the artichokes white. Peel and chop the onion.

Heat the butter in a saucepan and add the onion and drained artichokes. Add seasoning to taste. Cook gently for about 5 minutes, stirring occasionally. Do not let the artichokes brown. Slowly add the stock and bring to the boil. Simmer until the artichokes are very soft.

Rub the soup through a sieve, or blend it until smooth in a blender or food processor. Return the soup to the pan and stir in the milk. Bring to the boil, and serve.

MICHAEL FOOT
•
PARSNIP AND ORANGE SOUP

Ingredients
To serve 4 ✖✖✖

Metric/ Imperial		American
100 g/4 oz	parsnips	¼ lb
1	small onion	1
25 g/1 oz	butter	2 tbsp
1	orange	1
	salt and pepper	
Stock		
	veal or beef bones	
2	onions	2
2	large carrots	2
2–3	celery stalks	2–3
	fresh herbs, such as sage, mint, parsley, tarragon, or coriander.	

Method

First make the stock. Ask your butcher to give you a number of veal bones suitably cut up. Beef bones will do if no veal bones are obtainable. Place the bones in a large saucepan, or preferably a pressure cooker. Peel the onions and carrots and add to the pan with the celery, herbs and seasoning to taste. Cover with cold water and bring to the boil. Allow to simmer for several hours – the longer the better – unless in a pressure cooker in which case 30 minutes should be sufficient. Strain the liquid into a bowl and leave in the refrigerator overnight. By the morning, the fat will have risen to the top and can be lifted off, leaving a thick jellied stock.

If you prefer, chicken stock can be used in this recipe. To make this, boil a chicken instead of veal bones with the same ingredients as above. The boiled chicken can be used for all kinds of recipes, and the leftover strained stock can be retained as a basis for another soup.

Measure off 600 ml/1 pint (2½ cups) of the veal – or chicken – stock, and reserve the remainder for other uses.

Peel the parsnips and cut into very small pieces. Peel and thinly slice the onion. Heat the butter in a saucepan and cook the parsnips and onion until the onion is soft but not coloured.

Meanwhile, finely grate the rind from half of the orange. Squeeze the juice from the whole orange.

Add the orange rind and juice and the stock to the pan. Add seasoning to taste. Bring to the boil and simmer until the vegetables are very soft.

Blend the soup in a blender or food processor until smooth, or press it through a sieve. Reheat and serve.

IAN OGILVY
•
TURNIP AND ONION SOUP

Ingredients
To serve 4 ✗✗

Metric/ Imperial		American
1	large turnip	1
1	onion	1
1	garlic clove	1
75 g/3 oz	butter	6 tbsp
1 tbsp	flour	1 tbsp
1 tsp	curry powder	1 tsp
1.2 l/2 pints	beef stock	5 cups
	salt and pepper	
150 ml/¼ pint	single [light] cream	½ cup

Method

Peel and slice the turnip and onion. Peel and crush the garlic. Melt the butter in a saucepan, add the turnip, onion and garlic and stir to mix with the butter. Cover and sweat gently for 10 minutes.

Sprinkle the flour and curry powder over the vegetables and stir well. Gradually stir in the stock. Bring to the boil and simmer for 20 minutes.

Purée the soup in a blender or food processor, or pass it through a sieve. Return to the pan and reheat. Add salt and pepper to taste. Just before serving, stir in a little cream.

TED ROGERS
•
CREAM OF TOMATO SOUP

Ingredients
To serve 4–6 ✗✗

Metric/ Imperial		American
1	bacon slice or	1
25 g/1 oz	butter	2 tbsp
450 g/1 lb	tomatoes	1 lb
1	onion	1
1	carrot	1
1	celery stalk	1
900 ml/1½ pints	chicken stock	2 pints
1	bouquet garni	1
	salt and pepper	
25 g/1 oz	flour	2 tbsp
300 ml/½ pint	milk	1 cup
	sugar	
2 tbsp	chopped fresh parsley	2 tbsp
150 ml/¼ pint	cream (optional)	½ cup

Method

Chop the bacon. Slice the tomatoes. Peel and slice the onion and carrot. Chop the celery. Cook the bacon in a saucepan until it has rendered its fat; discard the bacon, reserving the fat. Alternatively, melt the butter in the pan. Add the tomatoes, onion, carrot and celery and cook for 2 minutes, stirring. Add the stock, bouquet garni and seasoning to taste. Bring to the boil, then simmer for 1 hour.

Rub the soup through a sieve and return it to the pan. Mix together the flour and milk and add to the pan. Bring to the boil, stirring well. Boil for 3 minutes. Stir in a pinch of sugar and the parsley. Taste and adjust the seasoning. A little cream may also be added, if liked. Serve hot.

17

JIMMY TARBUCK
•
VEGETABLE SOUP

Ingredients
To serve 6 ✗✗

Metric/ Imperial		American
1	leek	1
1	onion	1
¼	small head of cabbage	¼
700 g/1½ lb	potatoes	1½ lb
50 g/2 oz	beef dripping	¼ cup
1.8–2.4 l/3–4 pints	water	4–5 pints
	salt and pepper	
600 ml/1 pint	milk	2½ cups
1 tbsp	crushed tapioca	1 tbsp

Method

Wash and chop the leek. Peel and chop the onion. Chop the cabbage. Peel and slice the potatoes. Heat the dripping in a saucepan and add the prepared vegetables. Cook for a few minutes, then add the water and bring to the boil. Leave to simmer for about 1 hour.

Rub the soup through a sieve and return it to the pan. Add seasoning to taste. Bring back to the boil, then stir in the milk. Bring to the boil again and skim any scum from the top of the soup. Stir in the tapioca. Simmer for 10 minutes, stirring occasionally. Taste and adjust the seasoning before serving.

MIKE HARDING
•
ALLENSUPPE

Ingredients
To serve 4 ✗✗

Metric/ Imperial		American
2	large onions	2
2	garlic cloves	2
25 g/1 oz	butter	2 tbsp
1.8 l/3 pints	chicken stock	7½ cups
2	large carrots	2
4	large potatoes	4
1	medium swede [rutabaga]	1
2	celery stalks	2
3–4	tomatoes	3–4
1	medium potato	1
	salt and pepper	
450 g/1 lb	German garlic sausage	1 lb
	Worcestershire or Tabasco sauce (optional)	

Method

Peel the onions and chop them fairly small so that they will break down. Peel and crush the garlic. Take a large cast iron or other heavy pot and heat the butter in it until melted. Add the onions and garlic and cook until very soft and lightly browned. Then add your stock. If you have got any chicken stock from an old chicken that you have just massacred for Sunday dinner then you can use that. Otherwise use a bouillon cube if you have got one lying about handy, or if not just go out and knock a cow on the head, drag it back and bung it in the pot with everything else.

Peel and chop the carrots, large potatoes and swede [rutabaga]. Chop the celery and tomatoes. Grate the medium potato so it will cook down quickly and thicken the stock.

Add all the vegetables to the pot and cook them until they start to go soft. Just before it is ready, bung in a bit of salt and pepper and add the German garlic sausage, chopped into 2.5-cm/1-in cubes.

Ah, there is one point to remember. When you go to the shop make sure the assistant does not slice the sausage up into sandwich slices like they usually do. German garlic sausage is good, French garlic sausage will, in fact, do as a substitute but I have never found it works with the Swedish or Danish sausages which are very salty. Polish bola ring can be used as a substitute as well.

And that is just about it really. To give it a bit of zip you can add a couple of spoonfuls of Worcestershire sauce or a bit of Tabasco sauce. If you want to go right over the top, it is possible to get smoked beer from the Hamburg area in some German shops, and a cupful of that added just before the end makes the soup taste really nice indeed.

This does make a smashing tasty meal, particularly on a cold winter's afternoon – which is why I have never really understood why it is called German summer stew. Anyway, happy eating, or *frölich essen* or *gutten appetite* as they say in Germany!

19

PAUL McCARTNEY
•
GREEN PEA SOUP

Ingredients
To serve many ✖ ✖ ✖

Metric/ Imperial		American
700 g/1½ lb	green split peas	1½ lb
450 g/1 lb	orange lentils	1 lb
3	large onions	3
1	head of celery, including leaves	1
4	tomatoes	4
4	leeks	4
450 g/1 lb	butter or margarine	1 lb
	salt and pepper	

Method

Place the split peas and lentils in a large saucepan. Peel and quarter the onions and add to the pan. Clean the celery thoroughly and chop roughly. Add to the pan, with the leaves. Peel the tomatoes and add them. Thoroughly wash the leeks, chop them and add to the pan. Cover the ingredients with water, then add a further 900 ml/1½ pints [2 pints] water.

Bring to the boil and simmer for about 3 hours or until all the ingredients are very soft.

Add the butter or margarine and seasoning to taste. Stir and eat.

JON PERTWEE
•
THICK SPINACH SOUP

Ingredients
To serve 4 ✗ ✗

Metric/ Imperial		American
1 kg/2 lb	spinach	2 lb
300 ml/½ pint	chicken stock	1¼ cups
25 g/1 oz	butter	2 tbsp
2	eggs	2
3 tbsp	grated cheese	3 tbsp
	grated nutmeg	
	salt and pepper	

Method
Preheat the oven to 150°C/300°F/Gas 2.

Trim the spinach and rinse thoroughly. Place in a saucepan. There should be no need to add any water because there will be sufficient water clinging to the spinach leaves. Cook over a low heat for about 25 minutes or until very tender. If necessary, add a little more water to prevent sticking.

Drain the spinach. Put it into a casserole and add the stock and butter. Beat the eggs lightly with the cheese and add to the casserole. Add a generous pinch of nutmeg and seasoning to taste. Cook in the oven for 15 minutes, and serve hot.

'This is my favourite soup.' JON PERTWEE

COLD SOUPS

BILLY DAINTY
•
WATERCRESS SOUP

Ingredients
To serve 4 ✗ ✗

Metric/ Imperial		American
500 g/1 lb	potatoes	1 lb
1	onion	1
25 g/1 oz	butter	2 tbsp
	large bunch of watercress	
1	vegetable stock cube	1
	salt and pepper	
4 tbsp	single [light] cream	4 tbsp

Method
Peel the potatoes and cook in boiling water until tender.

Meanwhile, peel and finely chop the onion. Heat the butter in another saucepan, add the onion and cook until softened. Remove the stalks from the watercress and add the leaves to the onion. Cook until wilted.

Drain the potatoes, reserving the cooking liquid. Add the stock cube to the liquid and stir until dissolved.

Purée the potatoes, onion and watercress in a blender or food processor. Add the purée to the vegetable stock and stir well. Add salt and pepper to taste. Allow to cool, then chill.

Just before serving, stir in a little cream.

ESTHER RANTZEN
●
CONSOMMÉ PETTIFER

Ingredients
To serve 4–6 ✗✗✗

Metric/ Imperial		American
2 400-g/14-oz	cans of consommé	2 14-oz
150 ml/¼ pint	double [heavy] cream	¾ cup
4–6 tsp	caviar or lumpfish roe	4–6 tsp
4–6	lemon slices	4–6

Method
Chill the cans of consommé for at least 2 hours.

Divide the consommé, which will have set to a light jelly, between 4–6 serving bowls. Whip the cream until thick and put a dollop on each serving. Sprinkle the caviar on the cream. Garnish each serving with a slice of lemon.

CHRISTOPHER BIGGINS
●
VICHYSSOISE

Ingredients
To serve 6 ✗✗✗

Metric/ Imperial		American
2	medium leeks	2
1	small onion	1
25 g/1 oz	butter	2 tbsp
350 g/12 oz	floury potatoes	¾ lb
600 ml/1 pint	chicken stock	2½ cups
1	bouquet garni	1
¼ tsp	grated nutmeg	¼ tsp
	salt	
300 ml/½ pint	whipping cream	1¼ cups
2 tsp	chopped fresh chives, watercress or green part of leek	

Method
Wash the leeks thoroughly. Cut away and discard all the green part, then chop the white. Peel and thinly slice the onion. Heat the butter in a saucepan and cook the leeks and onion, covered, over a low heat until soft but not coloured. This will take about 15 minutes. Stir the vegetables occasionally to prevent them sticking.

Meanwhile, peel the potatoes and cut into chunks.

Add the potatoes to the saucepan with the stock, bouquet garni, nutmeg, and salt to taste. Bring to the boil, stirring occasionally, then cover and leave to simmer for 45 minutes.

Remove and discard the bouquet garni. Blend the soup, in two or three batches, to a smooth purée in a blender or food processor. Pour the soup into a bowl, cover and chill for at least 4 hours.

Before serving, gently whisk the cream into the soup. Ladle into bowls and sprinkle each serving with chives, watercress or green part of leek.

NIGEL HAWTHORNE
●
CHILLED AVOCADO SOUP

Ingredients
To serve 4 ✗✗

Metric/ Imperial		American
2	ripe avocados	2
1	garlic clove	1
	salt and pepper	
600 ml/1 pint	milk	2½ cups
4 tsp	chopped fresh chives, parsley or mint	4 tsp

Method
Cut the avocados in half and discard the stones. Scoop the flesh from the skins,

scraping the skins clean, and place the flesh in a blender or food processor. Peel and crush the garlic and add to the avocado with seasoning to taste. Blend to a thick, smooth pulp. Gradually add the milk, still blending.

Pour the soup into a bowl, cover tightly and chill for about 20 minutes. Serve sprinkled with chives, parsley or mint.

DEREK NIMMO
•
ICED CURRY CREAM SOUP

Ingredients
To serve 4–6 ✘ ✘ ✘

Metric/ Imperial		American
100 g/4 oz	shallots	¼ lb
25 g/1 oz	butter	2 tbsp
1 tbsp	curry paste	1 tbsp
25 g/1 oz	flour	2 tbsp
1 l/1¾ pints	vegetable or chicken stock	1 quart
1	strip of lemon rind	1
1	small bay leaf	1
2 tsp	arrowroot	2 tsp
1 tbsp	cold water	1 tbsp
Port cream		
120 ml/4 fl oz	port	½ cup
1 tsp	curry paste or powder	1 tsp
1½ tbsp	apricot jam or puréed dried apricots	1½ tbsp
2 tbsp	whipped cream or evaporated milk	2 tbsp

Method
Peel and finely chop the shallots. Heat about three-quarters of the butter in a saucepan and cook the shallots until softened. Add the curry paste and cook for 4–5 minutes, stirring frequently. Add the rest of the butter, then the flour and stir well. Pour in the stock and bring to the boil, stirring. Add the lemon rind and bay leaf. Simmer for 20 minutes.

Strain the soup and return it to the pan. Bring back to the boil. Dissolve the arrowroot in the cold water and add to the soup. Stir until thickened. Strain the soup again. Allow to cool, then chill.

To make the port cream, combine the port and curry paste or powder in a small saucepan. Stir well, then simmer until reduced to about half quantity. Allow to cool, then mix with the apricot jam or purée. Strain this mixture, then beat into the cream or evaporated milk.

Ladle the chilled soup into cups or bowls and add a spoonful of the port cream to each serving.

DOUGLAS FAIRBANKS JR.
•
HUNGARIAN YOGURT SOUP

Ingredients
To serve 4 ✘ ✘ ✘

Metric/ Imperial		American
450 ml/¾ pint	plain low-fat yogurt	2 cups
1	small garlic clove	1
4 tbsp	finely chopped cucumber	¼ cup
2 tbsp	finely chopped walnuts	2 tbsp
1 tbsp	good olive oil	1 tbsp
1 tbsp	chopped fresh dill	1 tbsp
	salt and white pepper	

Method
Place the yogurt in a mixing bowl. Peel and crush the garlic and add to the bowl with the cucumber, walnuts, oil, dill, and salt and pepper to taste. Beat lightly together.

Cover and chill for at least 3 hours or overnight. Stir thoroughly before serving.

JOHN DANKWORTH
•
GAZPACHO

Ingredients
To serve 4 ✗✗

Metric/Imperial		American
2	ripe tomatoes	2
1/2	large cucumber	1/2
1/2	sweet red or green pepper	1/2
1/2	Spanish or Bermuda onion	1/2
4	spring onions [scallions]	4
2	garlic cloves	2
40 g/1 1/2 oz	dry breadcrumbs	1/2 cup
	salt and pepper	
3 tbsp	olive oil	3 tbsp
2 tsp	white vinegar	2 tsp
350 ml/12 fl oz	cold water	1 1/2 cups
	ice cubes	
Garnish		
4 tbsp	finely chopped cucumber, onion, and tomato	4 tbsp
4	sliced hard-boiled eggs	4
4 tbsp	plain croûtons	4 tbsp

Method

Peel, seed and finely chop the tomatoes and cucumber. Core, seed and finely chop the sweet pepper. Peel or trim and finely chop all the onions. Place all the prepared vegetables in a large mixing bowl.

Peel the garlic and place it in a mortar. Add the breadcrumbs and seasoning to taste. Grind to a paste with the pestle. Add this paste to the vegetable mixture and stir to blend. Gradually stir in the oil and vinegar, then stir in 120 ml/4 fl oz [1/2 cup] of the cold water.

Put the remaining cold water in a large measuring jug and add enough ice cubes to bring the water level to 450 ml/3/4 pint [2 cups]. Pour this into the gazpacho and stir well. Cover and chill.

Before serving, remove any bits of ice. Garnish the soup and serve with French bread.

VEGETABLE APPETIZERS

LESLIE PHILLIPS
•
AVO DIP

Ingredients
To serve 4–6 ✗

Metric/ Imperial		American
2	avocados	2
1/2	onion	1/2
1	garlic clove	1
2 tbsp	cream	2 tbsp
1 tsp	sugar	1 tsp
1 dash	Tabasco sauce	1 dash
	juice of 1 lemon	
1 tsp	dried mixed herbs	1 tsp
	salt	

Method
Cut the avocados in half and discard the stones [pits]. Scoop out the flesh into a mixing bowl and mash it with a fork or spoon until smooth. Peel and grate the onion. Peel and crush the garlic. Add the onion and garlic to the avocado with the cream, a teaspoon of sugar, a dash of Tabasco sauce, and lemon juice, herbs, and salt to taste. Mix together well to make a soft dip.

Serve with savoury biscuits [crackers] or toast for dipping.

PAUL McDOWELL
•
AVOCADO MOUSSE

Ingredients
To serve 6–8 ✗✗✗

Metric/ Imperial		American
2	avocados	2
2 tbsp	lemon juice	2 tbsp
1 tbsp	finely chopped chives or spring onion [scallion] tops	1 tbsp
	salt and pepper	
1 sachet	unflavoured powdered gelatine	1 envelope
150 ml/1/4 pint	hot water	1/2 cup
4 tbsp	mayonnaise	1/4 cup
150 ml/1/4 pint	double [heavy] cream	1/2 cup
6–8	lemon slices	6–8
4 tbsp	parsley sprigs	4 tbsp

Method
Cut the avocados in half and discard the stones [pits]. Scoop out the flesh into a mixing bowl. Add the lemon juice, chives or spring onions [scallions] and seasoning to taste and mash with a fork or spoon until smooth and well blended.

Dissolve the gelatine in the hot water. Allow to cool, then stir into the avocado mixture. Fold in the mayonnaise. Whip the cream until thick and fold into the mixture.

Pour into a lightly oiled 900-ml/1½-pint [1-quart] mould and chill until set.

Turn out to serve, garnished with lemon slices and parsley sprigs. Serve with hot toast.

ALFRED MARKS
•
STUFFED MUSHROOMS

Ingredients
To serve 4 ✗✗

Metric/ Imperial		American
8	large cup mushrooms	8
2	lean bacon slices	2
75 g/3 oz	fine fresh breadcrumbs	1½ cups
½ tsp	dried mixed herbs	½ tsp
1	egg	1
	salt and pepper	
40 g/1½ oz	butter	3 tbsp
4	fried bread rounds to serve	4

Method
Preheat the oven to 180°C/350°F/Gas 4.

Remove the stalks from the mushroom caps. Set the caps aside. Chop the stalks finely and place in a mixing bowl. Finely chop the bacon, removing any rind first. Add to the bowl with the breadcrumbs, herbs, beaten egg, and seasoning to taste. Mix the ingredients together.

Stuff the mushroom caps with the mixture, doming up the stuffing. Arrange the stuffed mushrooms in a buttered baking dish and put a small piece of butter on top of each mushroom. Cover with buttered greaseproof [wax] paper. Bake for 15 minutes, then remove the paper and bake for a further 5 minutes.

Serve hot, on fried bread rounds. The mushrooms can also be served cold.

TERENCE ALEXANDER
•
BABA GANOUGE

Ingredients
To serve 4 ✗✗✗

Metric/ Imperial		American
4 175-g/6-oz	aubergines [eggplants]	4 6-oz
4	tomatoes	4
1	onion	1
1	sweet green pepper	1
2	garlic cloves	2
4–6 tbsp	olive oil	4–6 tbsp
2	lemons	2
1 tbsp	ground cumin	1 tbsp
½ tsp	cayenne pepper	½ tsp
	salt	
150 ml/¼ pint	tahina [sesame seed paste]	½ cup
4 tbsp	chopped fresh parsley	¼ cup

Method
Preheat the oven to 200°C/400°F/Gas 6.

Prick the aubergines [eggplants] here and there with a skewer. Bake them, whole and unpeeled, on a shelf in the oven until they are very soft to the touch. Allow to cool, then cut the aubergines [eggplants] in half and scoop out the flesh into a blender or food processor.

Peel and slice the tomatoes and onion. Core, seed and chop the green pepper. Peel and crush the garlic. Add the tomatoes, onion, green peppers, garlic, olive oil, juice of the lemons, cumin, cayenne, 1 tsp salt and the tahina to the aubergine [eggplant] flesh. Blend until smooth. Add half the parsley and blend again briefly just to mix.

Spoon the mixture into a serving dish and sprinkle over the remaining parsley. Serve with Arab pitta bread or savoury biscuits [crackers] for dipping.

FISH AND SHELLFISH

MILLICENT MARTIN
•
SMOKED SALMON DIP

Ingredients
To serve 8 ✗✗

Metric/ Imperial		American
225 g/8 oz	smoked salmon	½ lb
225 g/8 oz	cream cheese	½ lb
300 ml/½ pint	double [heavy] cream	1¼ cups
	juice of ½ lemon	
pinch	paprika	pinch
	pepper	
4 tsp	lumpfish or salmon roe	4 tsp

Method

Combine the salmon, cream cheese and cream in a blender or food processor. Blend until smooth. Add lemon juice, paprika and pepper to taste. If the dip is too thick, add a little more cream.

Spoon the dip into a bowl and sprinkle with lumpfish or salmon roe. Chill well before serving, with savoury biscuits [crackers].

DOROTHY TUTIN
•
SALMON MOUSSE WITH CUCUMBERED SOUR CREAM

Ingredients
To serve 4 ✗✗✗

Metric/ Imperial		American
150 ml/¼ pint	hot water	¾ cup
1 sachet	unflavoured powdered gelatine	1 envelope
1 tbsp	lemon juice	1 tbsp
200-g/7-oz	can of salmon or tuna	7-oz
2 tbsp	lightly whipped cream	2 tbsp
2 tbsp	mayonnaise	2 tbsp
	salt and pepper	
¼	small cucumber	¼
150 ml/¼ pint	sour cream	½ cup
	lemon wedges	
	cucumber slices to garnish	

Method

Put the hot water, gelatine and lemon juice in a blender and blend until the gelatine has dissolved. Drain the salmon or tuna and flake it lightly, discarding any bones. Add to the blender and blend until smooth.

Pour the mixture into a mixing bowl and add the cream and mayonnaise. Fold together. Add seasoning to taste. Pour into an oiled mould, cover and chill until set.

To make the sauce, peel the cucumber and remove the seeds, then chop the flesh finely. Add to the sour cream with seasoning to taste and stir to blend.

Turn out the mousse and serve with the sauce and lemon wedges, garnished with cucumber slices.

27

JAN LEEMING
●
MACKEREL MOUSSE

Ingredients
To serve 6–8 ✖✖✖

Metric/Imperial		American
1 15-oz	can of mackerel (Not in oil)	2 7-oz
2	celery stalks	2
1 tbsp	capers	1 tbsp
3 tbsp	water	3 tbsp
1 tbsp	wine vinegar	1 tbsp
1 tbsp	sugar	1 tbsp
1 tbsp (or one ¼-oz packet)	powdered gelatine (dissolved)	1 tsbp
1 tsp	dry mustard	1 tsp
	salt and black ground pepper to taste	
¼ pt	double cream (whipped)	¾ cup

Method

Put mackerel, finely sliced celery and capers in large bowl – mix well.

Put water, vinegar, sugar, mustard and dissolved gelatine into saucepan. Bring to boil and gently simmer for two minutes giving occasional stir. Put this mixture into bowl with other ingredients and stir.

Finally, add stiffly whipped cream to the mixture stirring well.

Rinse out a fish or ring mould with cold water. Spoon in the mixture and smooth the top. Cover and place in fridge to set – approximately six hours. Turn out of mould to serve.

If required, a layer of finely sliced tomato or cucumber can be placed in the bottom of the ring mould to provide decoration when turned out.

Variation: For a more splendid occasion substitute the mackerel with a can of salmon.

This dish freezes very well.

ROBIN BAILEY
•
MOULES MARINIÈRES

Ingredients
To serve 2 ✗ ✗

Metric/ Imperial		American
600 ml/1 pint	fresh mussels	1½ pints
1	onion	1
1	carrot	1
1	garlic clove	1
1	glass of white wine	1
1	bay leaf	1
1	fresh thyme sprig	1
1	small bunch of fresh parsley	1
	salt and pepper	
50 g/2 oz	butter	¼ cup
1 tbsp	flour	2 tbsp
2 tbsp	finely chopped fresh parsley	2 tbsp

Method
Scrub the mussels well and rinse them thoroughly. Put them in a deep pot with no more water than clings around the shells after washing. Peel and coarsely chop the onion and carrot. Peel and crush the garlic. Add these prepared ingredients to the pot with the wine, bay leaf, thyme, bunch of parsley, and pepper to taste. Cover and cook over a high heat for 10–15 minutes or until all the mussels are open (discard any that remain stubbornly closed).

Lift out the mussels and pull off the empty half shells. Do this over the pot so any liquid in the shells will be saved. Keep the mussels hot. Strain the cooking liquid and reserve.

Melt the butter in a saucepan and stir in the flour. Cook, stirring, until foaming but not coloured. Add the reserved cooking liquid and cook, stirring, until smooth and creamy. Add a goodly quantity of chopped parsley and correct the seasoning with a little salt (not too much) and pepper. Pour this sauce over the mussels and serve in soup plates. This is best accompanied by fresh French bread – and a finger bowl and napkin will be necessary!

RUSS ABBOT
•
ESCARGOTS BOURGUIGNONNE

Ingredients
To serve 4 ✗

Metric/ Imperial		American
225 g/8 oz	unsalted butter	1 cup
3	garlic cloves	3
1	lemon	1
2 tbsp	chopped fresh parsley	2 tbsp
	salt and pepper	
24	canned snails with shells	24
	French bread for serving	

Method
Preheat the oven to 230°C/450°F/Gas 8.

Beat the butter until softened. Peel and crush the garlic and add to the butter with the juice of the lemon, the parsley and salt and pepper to taste. Beat together well.

Put a blob of the butter mixture in each snail shell, then press in a snail. Stop up the opening in the shell with more butter. Arrange the snails on 4 heatproof dishes, preferably snail dishes.

Bake for 10–15 minutes or until piping hot and sizzling. Serve with lots of crusty French bread for dipping into the garlic butter.

BRYAN ROBSON
•
SAUTÉED KING PRAWNS

Ingredients
To serve 2–4 ✗

Metric/ Imperial		American
2 tbsp	cooking oil	2 tbsp
12	king prawns [jumbo shrimp] in shell	12
50 g/2 oz	butter	¼ cup
2 tbsp	dry white wine	2 tbsp
½	lemon	½
1	garlic clove	1
2 tbsp	chopped fresh parsley	2 tbsp
	salt and pepper	
1	lettuce, shredded	1
2–4	lemon wedges	2–4
2–4 tbsp	parsley sprigs to serve	2–4 tbsp

Method
Heat the oil in a frying pan. When hot, add the prawns and cook until the shells are golden brown, stirring frequently.

Drain off the oil. Add the butter to the pan and melt it. Add the wine, and juice of the ½ lemon. Peel and crush the garlic and add with the parsley and seasoning to taste. Simmer for 2–3 minutes.

Serve the prawns on a bed of lettuce, garnished with lemon wedges and parsley sprigs.

CILLA BLACK
•
SPECIAL PRAWN COCKTAIL

Ingredients
To serve 4 ✗✗

Metric/ Imperial		American
1	lettuce, shredded	1
4 tbsp	chopped cucumber	4 tbsp
225 g/8 oz	cooked peeled prawns [shrimp]	½ lb
1	small ripe melon	1
8	lemon wedges	8
Sauce		
6 tbsp	mayonnaise	6 tbsp
2 tbsp	tomato ketchup	2 tbsp
dash	Worcestershire sauce **or**	dash
1 tbsp	dry white wine	1 tbsp
1	small garlic clove (optional)	1

Method
First make the sauce. Mix the mayonnaise with enough tomato ketchup to give a pale pink colour. Add a dash of Worcestershire sauce, or for a very special flavour substitute dry white wine. Peel and crush the garlic and add it, if using.

Make a bed of lettuce and cucumber in four individual serving glasses. Arrange the prawns on top. Spoon over the sauce. Cover and chill for 45 minutes.

Halve the melon and discard the seeds. Scoop out the flesh in balls using a melon ball cutter, or peel the melon and cut the flesh into 1-cm/½-in cubes. Add the melon to the prawn cocktails and chill for a further 15 minutes.

Serve with lemon wedges.

Variation: use celery pieces instead of melon.

BERNARD CRIBBINS
●
SPICY PRAWNS

Ingredients
To serve 1 ✖

Metric/ Imperial		American
1 tbsp	cooking oil	1 tbsp
1	garlic clove	1
12	peeled cooked prawns [shrimp]	12
pinch/dash	cayenne pepper or Tabasco sauce	pinch/ dash

Method

Put the oil in a small earthenware dish (you eat from this as well). Heat the oil until very hot, then add the peeled garlic followed a few seconds later by the prawns and a pinch of cayenne pepper or a few drops of Tabasco sauce. Allow a little time for it all to get together and heat up, stirring occasionally, and serve with hot French bread.

JOHN MILLS
●
MANGO AND PRAWN COCKTAIL

Ingredients
To serve 4 ✖

Metric/ Imperial		American
2	ripe mangoes	2
225 g/8 oz	cooked peeled prawns [shrimp]	1/2 lb
100 g/4 oz	mayonnaise	1/2 cup
pinch	cayenne pepper	pinch

Method

Cut the mangoes in half lengthways. Carefully cut out the stone [seed] and discard it. Remove the mango flesh, leaving a thin layer on the skins. Chop the flesh and place it in a mixing bowl. Add the prawns and mayonnaise and fold together.

Pile the prawn mixture into the mango shells and sprinkle the tops with a little cayenne pepper.

JOHN MILLS

MIKE YARWOOD

•

SEAFOOD AU GRATIN

Ingredients
To serve 6 ✗✗

Metric/ Imperial		American
450 g/1 lb	potatoes	1 lb
75 g/3 oz	butter	6 tbsp
25 g/1 oz	flour	2 tbsp
450 ml/¾ pint	milk	2 cups
	salt and pepper	
75 g/3 oz	grated Cheddar cheese	¾ cup
2	hard-boiled eggs	2
2	tomatoes	2
100 g/4 oz	cooked peeled prawns [shrimp]	¼ lb
6 tbsp	parsley sprigs to garnish	6 tbsp

Method

Peel the potatoes. Place them in a saucepan, cover with water and bring to the boil. Simmer for about 20 minutes or until very tender.

Meanwhile, melt 25 g/1 oz [2 tbsp] of the butter in another saucepan and add the flour. Cook, stirring, for 1 minute, then gradually stir in the milk. Bring to the boil, stirring, and simmer until thickened. Add seasoning to taste. Stir in 50 g/2 oz [½ cup] of the cheese until melted. Remove the sauce from the heat and keep hot.

Preheat the grill [broiler].

Drain the potatoes and return them to the pan. Mash well, adding the remaining butter. Fork or pipe the mixture into a border in six scallop shells or individual ovenproof dishes.

Slice the hard-boiled eggs and tomatoes. Arrange in each potato 'nest'. Top with the prawns, reserving a few for the garnish. Spoon over the sauce and sprinkle the top with remaining cheese.

Place under the grill [broiler] and cook until the top is golden brown. Serve hot, garnished with the reserved prawns and parsley sprigs.

FRUIT STARTERS

NICHOLAS PARSONS
•
MELON AND TOMATO COCKTAIL

Ingredients
To serve 6 ✗✗✗

Metric/ Imperial		American
1	honeydew melon	1
3	large tomatoes	3
3	bananas	3
	juice of ½ lemon	
Herb mayonnaise		
1	large egg	1
1	egg yolk	1
1 tsp	caster [superfine] sugar	1 tsp
1 tsp	dry mustard	1 tsp
	salt and pepper	
300 ml/½ pint	cooking oil	1¼ cups
1–2 tbsp	white vinegar	1–2 tbsp
1 tbsp	chopped fresh mixed herbs or	1 tbsp
1 tsp	dried mixed herbs	1 tsp

Method
First make the mayonnaise. Combine the egg, egg yolk, sugar and mustard, and seasoning to taste in a mixing bowl. Add the oil, a drop at a time, beating well between each addition with a wooden spoon. As the mayonnaise starts to thicken, the oil can be added a little more quickly. When the mayonnaise is really thick, add the vinegar gradually until the sauce returns to the right consistency. Mix in the herbs. Cover and chill overnight.

The following day, cut the top off the melon about one-quarter of the way down. Trim the ends of both pieces so they will have flat bases. Discard the seeds. Using a melon ball cutter or teaspoon, scoop out the melon flesh from both pieces. Put the melon balls in a mixing bowl.

Peel and deseed the tomatoes. Cut them into wedges, and add to the bowl.

Slice the bananas and toss in lemon juice to prevent discoloration. Add to the bowl and fold together gently. Fill the large melon shell with the fruit mixture. Serve the herb mayonnaise in the melon lid.

GORDEN KAYE
•
PEARS IN TARRAGON CREAM

Ingredients
To serve 6 ✗✗

Metric/ Imperial		American
6	ripe dessert pears	6
300 ml/½ pint	double [heavy] cream	1¼ cups
2 tbsp	tarragon vinegar	2 tbsp
1 tbsp	caster [superfine] sugar	1 tbsp
	salt and pepper	

Method
Chill the pears. Whip together the cream, vinegar, and sugar, salt and pepper to taste. Chill this sauce also.

When ready to serve, peel the pears, cut them in half and scoop out the cores. Place two halves on each serving plate and top with a dollop of the tarragon cream.

33

PÂTÉS

JUDI DENCH
·
SMOKED MACKEREL PÂTÉ

Ingredients
To serve 4 ✖✖

Metric/ Imperial		American
225 g/8 oz	smoked mackerel fillets	½ lb
1	medium orange	1
4 tbsp	medium sweet cider	¼ cup
25 g/1 oz	melted butter	2 tbsp

Method
Remove any skin from the mackerel fillets and flake the flesh. Place it in a mixing bowl. Finely grate enough rind from the orange to make ½ tsp and add to the bowl with the juice of the orange, the cider and melted butter. Mix the ingredients together thoroughly. (This may be done in a blender or food processor for a smoother result.)

Pack the pâté into a small pot and chill until firm. Serve with toast, French bread or Melba toast.

BOB LANGLEY
·
ROUGH STYLE PÂTÉ

Ingredients
To serve 6 or more ✖✖✖

Metric/ Imperial		American
100 g/4 oz	mushrooms	¼ lb
1	medium onion	1
15 g/½ oz	butter	1 tbsp
405 g/1 lb	green (unsmoked) bacon	1 lb
450 g/1 lb	calf's, lamb's or pig's liver	1 lb
1 tsp	grated nutmeg	1 tsp
1	large egg	1
	salt and pepper	
1 tbsp	dried thyme	1 tbsp

Method
Preheat the oven to 300°F/150°C/Gas 2.

Finely chop the mushrooms. Peel and finely chop the onion. Heat the butter in a small pan and cook the mushrooms and onion until the onion is soft but not brown. Remove from the heat.

Mince [grind] the bacon and liver and place in a mixing bowl. Add the mushrooms and onion, the nutmeg, beaten egg, and seasoning to taste. Mix well. Pack the mixture into a greased ovenproof dish and sprinkle the thyme over the surface. Cover the dish with foil. Bake for 3 hours.

Allow to cool completely, still covered with foil. When cold, beat the mixture thoroughly and pack it into a 450 g/1 lb loaf pan. Cover again and chill before serving. If not for immediate use, the pâté may also be frozen.

PAUL DANIELS
●
LIVER PÂTÉ

Ingredients
To serve 6–8 ✖✖✖

Metric/ Imperial		American
25 g/1 oz	butter	2 tbsp
25 g/1 oz	flour	2 tbsp
150 ml/¼ pint	milk	¾ cup
2 tsp	finely chopped onion	2 tsp
3 tbsp	cream	3 tbsp
225 g/8 oz	bacon	½ lb
450 g/1 lb	lamb's or pig's liver	1 lb
2	eggs	2
1	garlic glove (optional)	1
½ tsp	sugar	½ tsp
	salt and pepper	
2 tbsp	brandy (optional)	2 tbsp
100 g/4 oz	bacon slices	¼ lb
	gherkins, parsley and lemon to garnish	

Method

Preheat the oven to 180°C/350°F/Gas 4.

Melt the butter in a saucepan and stir in the flour. Cook, stirring, for 1 minute, then gradually stir in the milk to make a thick sauce. Stir in the onion and cream. (Choose thick cream for a rich pâté, thin cream for a light pâté.) Remove from the heat and set aside.

Mince [grind] the bacon and liver coarsely. Or, for a smoother, creamier pâté, put them through the mincer [grinder] twice. Put the bacon and liver in a mixing bowl and add the sauce and eggs. Peel and crush the garlic, if using. Add it to the bowl with the sugar, seasoning to taste and the brandy if an extra special pâté is wanted. Mix well together.

Press the mixture firmly into a greased shallow dish and arrange the bacon slices across the top. Stand the dish in a baking pan partly filled with cold water and bake for about 1 hour. Allow to cool completely.

Garnish with gherkins, parsley and lemon, and serve with hot toast.

FISH
AND
SHELLFISH

MAIN
COURSES

OLIVIA HUSSEY
•
SASHIMI

Ingredients
To serve 4 ✖✖✖

Metric/ Imperial		American
450 g/1 lb	fresh fish such as salmon, tuna, squid	1 lb
	handful of fresh dill, parsley, watercress or other herb	
2 tsp	grated horseradish or green mustard (wasabi powder)	2 tsp
4 tbsp	soy sauce	¼ cup
	capers (optional)	
Marinated bean sprouts		
450 g/1 lb	fresh bean sprouts	1 lb
3 tbsp	chopped spring onions [scallions], green and white parts	3 tbsp
2 tbsp	sesame seed oil	2 tbsp
2 tbsp	soy sauce	2 tbsp
1 tbsp	vodka	1 tbsp
1 tbsp	vinegar	1 tbsp

Method

First prepare the bean sprouts. Place them in a colander and immerse it in a large saucepan of boiling water. Remove the colander from the water and drain. Immediately rinse the sprouts with cold water. Drain.

Combine the remaining ingredients in a large mixing bowl. Add the bean sprouts and toss to mix. Leave to marinate at room temperature for 1 hour, then chill for at least 3 hours before serving.

Slice the fish and arrange on a platter with the herbs or watercress. Mix the horseradish or green mustard with the soy sauce to make a dipping sauce. If liked, garnish the fish with capers. Serve with the marinated bean sprouts.

'This is my favourite Japanese recipe. It should be accompanied by marinated bean sprouts. It is very low in calories, delicious and very high in energy.' OLIVIA HUSSEY

37

RICHARD BAKER
·
FISH CRUMBLE

Ingredients
To serve 4 ✗✗

Metric/ Imperial		American
350 g/12 oz	white fish steaks or fillets	¾ lb
350 g/12 oz	smoked fish fillets	¾ lb
450 ml/¾ pint	milk	2 cups
90 g/3½ oz	butter or margarine	7 tbsp
140 g/5½ oz	flour	1 cup + 3 tbsp
100 g/4 oz	grated Cheddar cheese	1 cup
	salt and pepper	

Method
Preheat the oven to 180°C/350°F/Gas 4.

Place the fish in an ovenproof dish and pour over the milk. Bake for about 20 minutes or until the fish is cooked. Alternatively, the fish may be poached in the milk on top of the stove.

Drain the fish, reserving the milk. Flake the fish, discarding all skin and bones, and set aside.

Measure the reserved milk: add a little more fresh milk to make 300 ml/½ pint [1¼ cups] if necessary. Melt 40 g/1½ oz [3 tbsp] of the butter in a saucepan and add 40 g/1½ oz [3 tbsp] of the flour. Cook, stirring, for 1 minute, then gradually stir in the milk. Simmer, stirring, until thickened. Add half the cheese and seasoning to taste and stir until the sauce is smooth.

Add the fish to the sauce and stir to mix. Pour into an ovenproof dish.

Rub the remaining butter into the remaining flour until the mixture resembles breadcrumbs. Rub in the remaining cheese. Sprinkle this crumble over the fish mixture. Bake for about 30 minutes or until the top is golden brown.

COLIN BAKER
·
JANSSON'S TEMPTATION

Ingredients
To serve 4 ✗✗

Metric/ Imperial		American
8	medium potatoes	8
2	large onions	2
2 50-g/2-oz	cans of anchovy fillets	2 2-oz
	pepper	
150 ml/¼ pint	double [heavy] cream	¾ cup
50 g/2 oz	fresh breadcrumbs	1 cup
25 g/1 oz	butter	2 tbsp

Method
Preheat the oven to 200°C/400°F/Gas 6.

Peel the potatoes and cut into thin slices. Peel and chop the onions. Drain the anchovies. In a buttered ovenproof dish, make alternative layers of the potatoes, onions and anchovies, beginning with onion and ending with potatoes. Season the layers with pepper to taste. Pour over the cream. Sprinkle the breadcrumbs on top and dot with pieces of butter.

Bake for about 50 minutes or until the potatoes are tender. Serve hot.

DON ESTELLE
●
SHRIMP POTATO BALLS

Ingredients
Makes about 24 ✗✗

Metric/ Imperial		American
500 g/1 lb	hot mashed potatoes	2 cups
2 tsp	butter	2 tsp
4 tbsp	grated Parmesan cheese	1/4 cup
1 tbsp	lemon juice	1 tbsp
1 tbsp	finely chopped fresh parsley	1 tbsp
100 g/4 oz	peeled cooked shrimps	1/4 lb
1–2	eggs	1–2
	salt and pepper	
75 g/3 oz	fresh breadcrumbs	1 1/2 cups
	oil for deep frying	

Method

Put the mashed potatoes in a bowl and add the butter, Parmesan cheese, lemon juice and parsley. If the shrimps are large, cut them in half and add to the bowl. Lightly beat the eggs and add just enough to give the mixture a soft but manageable consistency. Add salt and pepper to taste.

Shape the mixture into walnut-size balls. Coat in the remaining beaten egg and then with breadcrumbs.

Heat the oil for deep frying to 190°C/375°F.

Deep fry the shrimp balls, a few at a time to prevent crowding, for 3 1/2–4 minutes or until golden brown and crisp. Drain on paper towels and serve hot, with a mixed salad.

BETTY DRIVER
●
SALMON KEDGEREE

Ingredients
To serve 5 ✗

Metric/ Imperial		American
200 g/7 oz	long-grain rice	1 cup
	salt and pepper	
200-g/7-oz	can of red salmon or	7-oz
225 g/8 oz	cooked fresh salmon fillet	1/2 lb
50 g/2 oz	butter	1/4 cup
2	hard-boiled eggs	2
3 tbsp	double [heavy] cream	3 tbsp
pinch	cayenne pepper	pinch
2 tbsp	chopped fresh parsley	2 tbsp

Method

Cook the rice in boiling salted water until tender.

Meanwhile, drain the can of salmon. Flake the fish, removing any bits of bone or cartilage. If using fresh salmon, flake it, removing all skin and bone.

Heat the butter in a saucepan and add the fish. Finely chop the hard-boiled eggs and add to the pan with the cream and cayenne, salt and pepper to taste. Stir until piping hot.

Drain the rice, if necessary, and add to the fish mixture. Fold together gently. Mix in the parsley. Turn onto a heated serving dish and shape into a pyramid with a fork. Serve hot.

Variation: Use smoked cod instead of salmon, and add 1/2 onion, peeled and thinly sliced, lightly fried first in the butter.

'This is a lovely supper dish and doesn't require anything else with it. We eat this a lot as we don't eat meat.'
BETTY DRIVER

LESLIE GRANT
•
MARINARA

Ingredients
To serve 4–6 ✖

Metric/ Imperial		American
450 g/1 lb	cooked king prawns [jumbo shrimp] in shell	1 lb
225 g/8 oz	fresh scallops	½ lb
50-g/2-oz	can of anchovy fillets	2-oz
150 ml/¼ pint	dry white wine	½ cup
150 ml/¼ pint	water	½ cup
5	large ripe tomatoes or	5
400-g/14-oz	can of tomatoes	16-oz
2	garlic cloves	2
2 tbsp	cooking oil	2 tbsp
1 tbsp	tomato purée [paste]	1 tbsp
8	fresh shelled [shucked] oysters	8
1 tbsp	chopped fresh parsley	1 tbsp
1 tbsp	chopped fresh mint (optional)	1 tbsp
	salt and pepper	

Method
Peel and devein the prawns. Cut the scallops in half if they are large. Drain the anchovies and pat dry with paper towels.

Place the wine and water in a saucepan and bring to the boil. Add the scallops and cook for 1 minute. Drain and set aside.

Peel and chop the tomatoes, or drain canned tomatoes. Peel and crush the garlic. Heat the oil in a pan and add the tomatoes, garlic and tomato purée [paste]. Cook, stirring, for 2 minutes. Add all the seafood and cook for a further 1 minute. Stir in the parsley and mint, if using, and add seasoning to taste. Serve hot, spooned over pasta.

DON MacLEAN
•
CRAB QUICHE

Ingredients
To serve 4 ✖✖

Metric/ Imperial		American
100 g/4 oz	shortcrust [pie] pastry for 20-cm/8-in pie pan	1 cup
1	beaten egg to glaze	1
25 g/1 oz	butter	2 tbsp
225 g/8 oz	cooked crabmeat	½ lb
2 tbsp	finely chopped fresh parsley	2 tbsp
2 tbsp	dry sherry	2 tbsp
4	egg yolks	4
300 ml/½ pint	single [light] cream	1¼ cups
pinch	grated nutmeg	pinch
	salt and pepper	

Method
Roll out the pastry and use to line the pie pan. Prick the bottom with a fork, then chill for 30 minutes.

Preheat the oven to 190°C/375°F/Gas 5.

Brush the pastry case with beaten egg. Bake blind for 15 minutes.

Meanwhile, heat the butter in a small pan and sauté the crabmeat and parsley until just beginning to brown. Stir in the sherry.

Fill the pastry case with the crab mixture. Lightly beat the egg yolks in a mixing bowl, then beat in the cream until the mixture is thick and lemon coloured. Add nutmeg, salt and pepper to taste. Pour over the crab mixture.

Reduce the oven temperature to 180°C/350°F/Gas 4. Bake the quiche for about 30 minutes. Serve hot or cold.

BILLY CONNOLLY
●
STUFFED TROUT

Ingredients
To serve 2 ✖✖

Metric/ Imperial		American
2	fresh trout, preferably brown	2
2	peeled and chopped tomatoes	2
1 tsp	chopped fresh basil	1 tsp
2 tsp	ground walnuts and almonds	2 tsp
2	hard-boiled eggs	2
1 tbsp	chopped spring onions [scallions]	1 tbsp

Method
Preheat the oven to 180°C/350°C/Gas 4.

Have the trout cleaned or do this yourself. Rinse and pat dry. To make the stuffing, combine the tomatoes, basil and nuts. The consistency is up to yourself, but I like it to be like a thick, stiffish paste. Stuff the trout with the mixture and wrap each fish in a piece of lightly greased foil. Bake for 50 minutes.

Just before the fish is ready, mash the hard-boiled eggs with the spring onions [scallions]. Serve this with the trout.

'May your tastebuds dance a wild jig!' BILLY CONNOLLY

GERAINT EVANS
●
TROUT WITH ALMONDS

Ingredients
To serve 2 ✖✖

Metric/ Imperial		American
2	rainbow trout, cleaned	2
100 g/4 oz	butter	1/2 cup
1/2	lemon	1/2
	salt and pepper	
50 g/2 oz	flaked almonds	1/2 cup
150 ml/1/4 pint	single [light] cream	1/2 cup
1 tbsp	chopped fresh parsley to garnish	1 tbsp

Method
Preheat the grill [broiler] to moderate.

Remove the fins from the trout. Rinse the fish and pat dry.

Place the butter in the grill [broiler] pan and heat it under the grill [broiler] until melted. Lay the trout in the melted butter and turn to coat on all sides. Squeeze over the juice of the 1/2 lemon and add seasoning to taste. Sprinkle with the almonds. Place the trout under the heat and cook for 8 minutes, turning once.

Remove the trout and almonds from the grill [broiler] pan and keep hot. Add the cream to the melted butter in the pan and return to the heat. Allow the mixture to heat through until it thickens.

Arrange the trout on a serving dish and spoon over the cream sauce. Garnish with the toasted almonds and chopped parsley and serve hot.

MICHAEL ASPEL
●
FILLETS OF SOLE MEURAT

Ingredients
To serve 4 ✗✗

Metric/ Imperial		American
750 g/1½ lb	*sole fillets, skinned*	*1½ lb*
2	*potatoes*	*2*
2	*cooked artichoke bottoms*	*2*
225 g/8 oz	*ripe tomatoes*	*½ lb*
	salt and pepper	
2 tbsp	*flour for coating*	*2 tbsp*
100 g/4 oz	*butter*	*½ cup*
2 tbsp	*olive oil*	*2 tbsp*
3 tbsp	*chopped fresh parsley*	*3 tbsp*
1	*lemon*	*1*

Method

Cut the sole fillets crossways into strips. Peel and dice the potatoes. Dice the artichoke bottoms. Peel, seed and chop the tomatoes. Sprinkle the tomatoes with salt and pepper to taste.

Coat the sole fillet strips with flour, shaking off any excess. Melt 25 g/1 oz [2 tbsp] of the butter in a frying pan, add about half of the sole strips and cook until lightly browned on all sides. As the sole strips are browned, remove them from the pan. Cook the remaining sole strips in the same way, adding another 25 g/1 oz [2 tbsp] of butter to the pan. Set the sole aside and keep warm.

Melt another 25 g/1 oz [2 tbsp] of butter in the pan and add the potato dice. Cook briskly, stirring frequently, until tender and beginning to brown. Add the artichoke dice and cook for a further 2–3 minutes.

Meanwhile, heat the oil in another frying pan. Add the tomatoes and cook for about 5 minutes or until the excess liquid has evaporated.

Add the sole strips to the potato and artichoke mixture and cook, stirring frequently, for 2–3 minutes longer.

Transfer the tomato to a warmed serving dish. Arrange the sole, potato and artichoke mixture on top. Keep hot.

Melt the remaining butter in a small saucepan and cook until it turns nut brown. Do not let it brown too much and burn.

Pour the butter over the fish mixture. Sprinkle with parsley and a good squeeze of lemon juice and serve.

GEOFF LEWIS
•
VELOUTÉ MIGNON

Ingredients
To serve 6 ✖ ✖

Metric/ Imperial		American
100 g/4 oz	carrot	1/4 lb
100 g/4 oz	onion	1/4 lb
100 g/4 oz	celery	1/4 lb
1/2	garlic clove	1/2
100 g/4 oz	scallops	1/4 lb
100 g/4 oz	sole fillets	1/4 lb
25 g/1 oz	butter	2 tbsp
600 ml/1 pint	boiling fish stock	2 1/2 cups
150 ml/1/2 pint	dry white wine	1/2 cup
300 ml/1/2 pint	double [heavy] cream	1 cup
1	bay leaf	1
	salt and pepper	
100 g/4 oz	cooked peeled prawns [bay shrimp]	1/4 lb
100 g/4 oz	cooked peeled scampi [jumbo shrimp]	1/4 lb

Method

Peel the carrot and onion. Cut the carrot, onion and celery into matchstick strips about 2.5 cm/1 inch long. Peel and finely chop the garlic. Cut the scallops and sole into strips.

Melt the butter in a large wide pan and add the carrot, onion, celery and garlic. Cook until softened but not brown. Remove the vegetables with a slotted spoon and set aside.

Add the sole and scallops to the pan and cook until just tender without allowing to brown. Remove the fish with a slotted spoon and set aside.

Add the fish stock, wine, cream and bay leaf and bring to the boil. Boil until reduced and saucelike. Discard the bay leaf. Add salt and pepper to taste.

Return the vegetables, sole and scallops to the pan and add the prawns and scampi [shrimp]. Stir to mix with the sauce. Heat through gently (do not overcook or the shellfish will be tough), and serve hot.

43

DONALD PLEASANCE
•
SOLE BONNE FEMME

Ingredients
To serve 2 ✗✗

Metric/ Imperial		American
1	large sole	1
250 ml/8 fl oz	water	1 cup
	salt and pepper	
40 g/1½ oz	butter	3 tbsp
2	shallots	2
225 g/8 oz	button mushrooms	½ lb
250 ml/8 fl oz	dry white wine	1 cup
1	bouquet garni	1
12	mushroom caps	12
2 tbsp	olive oil	2 tbsp
	lemon juice	
2 tbsp	flour	2 tbsp

Method

Fillet the sole. Set the fillets aside, and put the skin, bones and any trimmings in a saucepan with the water. Bring to the boil and simmer for 10 minutes. Strain this fish stock. Add salt and pepper to taste and set aside.

Preheat the oven to 180°C/350°F/Gas 4.

Grease an earthenware baking dish with 15 g/½ oz [1 tbsp] of the butter. Put the sole fillets in the dish. Peel and finely chop the shallots and sprinkle over the fish. Finely chop the button mushrooms and scatter over the top. Add enough wine just to cover the fish and add the fish stock. Tuck in the bouquet garni. Bring to the boil on top of the stove, then cover with buttered greaseproof paper and transfer to the oven. Bake for 10 minutes.

Meanwhile, sauté the mushrooms caps in the olive oil until golden brown. Add a squeeze of lemon juice and keep hot.

Drain off the liquid from the baking dish into a saucepan. Add the remaining wine and bring to the boil. Blend the remaining butter with the flour to make a smooth paste. Add this in small balls to the boiling cooking liquid, stirring, and simmer until thickened. Taste and adjust the seasoning.

Pour the sauce over the sole and serve garnished with the mushroom caps.

MARTI CAINE
•
SOLE WITH PRAWNS

Ingredients
To serve 4 ✗✗

Metric/ Imperial		American
8	skinless sole fillets	8
150 ml/¼ pint	dry white wine	½ cup
150 ml/¼ pint	fish stock or water	½ cup
	lemon juice	
	salt and pepper	
65 g/2½ oz	butter	5 tbsp
50 g/2 oz	flour	¼ cup
150 ml/¼ pint	milk	½ cup
150 ml/¼ pint	double [heavy] cream	½ cup
½ tsp	grated nutmeg	½ tsp
175 g/6 oz	cooked peeled prawns [shrimp]	6 oz
100 g/4 oz	button mushrooms	1 cup
	lemon slices and parsley sprigs to garnish	

Method

Preheat the oven to 160°C/325°F/Gas 3.

Roll up each sole fillet and arrange in one layer in a buttered ovenproof dish. Pour over the wine, fish stock or water, a little lemon juice, and seasoning to taste. Bake for about 20 minutes.

Meanwhile, heat 50 g/2 oz [½ cup] of the butter in a saucepan and add the flour. Cook, stirring, for 1 minute. Gradually stir in the milk and cream. Drain the liquid from the fish and add to the sauce; keep the fish hot. Simmer the sauce, stirring, until it is thick and smooth. Add the nutmeg, prawns and seasoning to taste. Remove from the heat and keep hot.

Heat the remaining butter in a small pan and fry the mushrooms until just beginning to brown. Stir the mushrooms into the sauce.

Arrange the fish rolls on a warmed serving dish and pour over the sauce. Garnish with lemon slices and parsley sprigs and serve hot.

NORMAN TEBBIT
•
MUSSELS IN WINE CREAM

Ingredients
To serve 4 ✗✗

Metric/ Imperial		American
1	shallot	1
1	small bunch of fresh parsley	1
	few celery leaves	
50 g/2 oz	butter	¼ cup
250 ml/8 fl oz	dry white wine	1 cup
3 l/5 pints	mussels	3 quarts
250 ml/8 fl oz	double [heavy] cream	1 cup
	salt and pepper	
2 tbsp	chopped fresh parsley	2 tbsp

Method

Peel and coarsely chop the shallot. Coarsely chop the parsley and celery leaves. Melt half the butter in a wide pan and add the shallot, parsley, celery leaves and wine. Bring to the boil.

Scrub the mussels well and add to the pan. Cover and cook for 3–5 minutes or until the mussel shells open. Transfer the mussels to a warmed serving dish or tureen, pouring the liquor from their shells back into the pan. Discard any mussels that remain closed. Keep the opened mussels warm.

Strain the cooking liquid through muslin and return it to the pan. Add the cream and stir to mix. Bring to the boil and boil until the mixture is reduced and saucelike. Remove from the heat and swirl in the remaining butter. Add salt and pepper to taste, and stir in the chopped parsley.

Pour the sauce over the mussels and serve immediately.

MEAT MAIN COURSES

BEEF

BOBBY ROBSON
•
BEEF WELLINGTON

Ingredients
To serve 4–6 ✗✗

Metric/ Imperial		American
1	fillet [tenderloin] of beef	1
2 tbsp	olive oil	2 tbsp
	smooth liver pâté or pâté de foie gras	
225 g/8 oz	puff pastry	½ lb
1	beaten egg to glaze	1

Method

Weigh the fillet: you will need about 100 g/ 4 oz pâté for every 500 g/1 lb of beef.

Heat the oil in a frying pan, add the beef and brown quickly on all sides. Remove the beef to paper towels, and leave to drain and cool.

Preheat the oven to 220°C/425°F/Gas 7.

Spread the pâté over one side of the beef fillet.

Roll out the puff pastry to an oblong large enough to wrap around the beef. Place the beef on the pastry, pâté side down, and wrap the pastry round. Brush the edges with beaten egg and press firmly to seal. Trim off any excess pastry.

Place the pastry-wrapped beef on a baking sheet, seam side down. Prick the top and decorate with the pastry trimmings, if liked. Brush with beaten egg.

Bake, allowing about 20 minutes for every 500 g/1 lb of beef, until the pastry is puffed and golden brown. The beef will be rare. Serve hot.

'My favourite meal would be smoked salmon, beef Wellington and Brie or Camembert cheese.' BOBBY ROBSON

47

DAVID JACOBS

ROAST BEEF WITH YORKSHIRE PUDDING

Ingredients

To serve 4–6 ✖✖✖

Metric/ Imperial		American
	piece of beef for roasting	
	salt and pepper	
100 g/4 oz	flour	1 cup
1	egg	1
300 ml/½ pint	milk or milk and water mixed	1½–1¾ cups
15–25 g/ ½–1 oz	fat	1–2 tbsp

Method

Preheat the oven to 220°C/425°F/Gas 7.

Season the meat lightly. If it is a very lean cut, it should be larded with fat to keep it moist during roasting. Meat that has been boned should be tied into a neat shape with string.

Roast the beef for 45 minutes, then reduce the heat to 200°C/400°F/Gas 6 and continue roasting. If you like your beef rare, allow 15 minutes cooking time to each 450 g/ 1 lb, with 15 minutes extra; for medium-done beef allow 20 minutes cooking time to each 450 g/1 lb, with 20 minutes extra; and for well-done beef allow 25 minutes cooking time to each 450 g/1 lb, with 25 minutes extra. If you are using a covered roasting pan, or wrapping the beef in foil, allow an extra 20 minutes cooking time.

To prepare the Yorkshire pudding, sift the flour into a mixing bowl with a pinch of salt. Break in the egg and beat well, then beat in enough milk, or mixed milk and water, to give a stiff batter. Allow to stand for a few minutes, then gradually beat in the remainder of the liquid.

Rub individual patty tins with the fat, or put the fat in a larger baking pan and melt in the oven. Pour the batter into the tins or pan and bake. Individual puddings need about 20 minutes in all; a large pudding takes a bit longer.

If you are baking the puddings in a separate oven, start them off at 230°C/450°F/ Gas 8, then after 10 minutes reduce the heat to 220°C/425°F/Gas 7 for the rest of the time.

'My favourite meal is Sunday lunch, and nothing pleases me more than roast beef, Yorkshire pudding, roast potatoes and green beans, followed by raspberries and double cream. Could there be anything lovelier, especially if the beef is Aberdeen Angus and all the fruit and vegetables are home grown?' DAVID JACOBS

TREVOR FRANCIS
•
STEAK ARGENTINE

Ingredients
To serve 4 ✗✗

Metric/ Imperial		American
4	beef steaks	4
1	egg	1
	salt and pepper	
4 tbsp	fresh breadcrumbs	4 tbsp
	oil for deep frying	
4	slices of cooked ham	4
4	slices of cheese	4
2	sliced tomatoes	2

Method
Dip the steaks into the egg which has been beaten with seasoning to taste, then coat them in breadcrumbs. Deep fry until the steaks are golden brown on all sides and done to your taste. Drain well on paper towels.

Preheat the grill [broiler].

Place a slice of ham and a slice of cheese on top of each steak. Cook under the grill [broiler] for a few minutes until the cheese has melted and is lightly browned. Top each serving with sliced tomatoes and serve.

EDDIE LARGE
•
STEAK À LA EDDIE

Ingredients
To serve 4 ✗✗

Metric/ Imperial		American
1	onion	1
100 g/4 oz	butter	½ cup
100 g/4 oz	mushrooms	1 cup
450 ml/¾ pint	double [heavy] cream	2 cups
300 ml/½ pint	beef stock	1¼ cups
4 175-g/6-oz	steaks such as sirloin, rump, etc.	4 6-oz
	flour for dredging	
	salt and pepper	
4	potatoes	4

Method
Peel and finely chop the onion. Heat half the butter in a saucepan and cook the onion until soft but not brown. Slice the mushrooms and add to the pan. Stir in the cream and stock and leave to cook while you brown the meat.

Flour the steaks lightly on all sides and season to taste. Heat the remaining butter in a frying pan and fry the steaks over a high heat until browned on both sides. Add the mushroom cream mixture. Reduce the heat, cover the pan and cook for 30 minutes, turning the steaks occasionally.

Peel and dice the potatoes. Add to the pan and cook for a further 30 minutes. Taste and adjust the seasoning before serving.

KEN DODD
•
STEAK DIANE

Ingredients
To serve 4 ✗✗

Metric/ Imperial		American
450 g/1 lb	rump or sirloin steak	1 lb
1	small onion	1
1	lemon	1
100 g/4 oz	unsalted butter	½ cup
	Worcestershire sauce	
1 tbsp	chopped fresh parsley	1 tbsp
2 tsp	sugar	2 tsp
3 tbsp	brandy	3 tbsp

Method

Cut the steak into four portions. Trim off all fat and gristle, then beat the steaks with a meat pounder or mallet or a rolling pin until they are very thin. Peel and chop the onion. Finely grate the rind from the lemon, and squeeze out the juice.

Heat half the butter in a frying pan and cook the onion until softened. Remove the onion with a slotted spoon and set aside.

Heat the fat in the pan and add two of the steaks. Fry over high heat until browned on both sides. Remove from the pan. Add the remaining butter to the pan, then brown the remaining two steaks.

Return the onion to the pan and add a few drops of Worcestershire sauce, the lemon rind and juice, parsley, and sugar. Stir well. Return the steaks to the pan and turn to coat with the sauce. Add the brandy and heat it, then set it alight. As soon as the flames die down, serve the steaks with the sauce poured over them.

DEREK BATEY
•
BEEF SAUTÉ CHASSEUR

Ingredients
To serve 4–6 ✗✗✗

Metric/ Imperial		American
900 g/2 lb	porterhouse, rump or skirt steak	2 lb
3	shallots or	3
1	small onion	1
1	garlic clove	1
2 tbsp	cooking oil	2 tbsp
40 g/1½ oz	butter	3 tbsp
1 tbsp	flour	1 tbsp
300–450 ml/ ½–¾ pint	rich brown stock	1¼–2 cups
	salt and pepper	
225 g/8 oz	button mushrooms	½ lb
2	glasses of white wine	2
1 tbsp	tomato purée [paste]	1 tbsp
2 tbsp	chopped fresh parsley to garnish	2 tbsp

Method
Cut the meat into 5-cm/2-in cubes, discarding all fat and gristle. Peel and finely chop the shallots or onion and the garlic. Heat the oil in a shallow stew pan or sauté pan and when hot, drop in 25 g/1 oz [2 tbsp] of the butter. Fry the cubes of meat a few at a time until nicely browned on all sides. As the meat is browned, remove it from the pan.

Reduce the heat and add the shallots or onion and garlic. Cook until soft. Sprinkle over the flour and cook, stirring, until a rich russet-brown. Remove the pan from the heat and blend in the stock. Return to the heat and bring to the boil, stirring well. Return the meat to the pan with seasoning to taste. Cover and simmer for about 45 minutes or until tender.

Quarter the mushrooms if they are large;
if small, leave them whole. Heat the remaining butter in a frying pan and cook the mushrooms for about 2 minutes. Add the wine and bring to the boil. Boil hard until reduced by half. Stir in the tomato purée [paste].

Add the mushroom mixture to the meat and continue cooking for about 10 minutes.

Serve hot, sprinkled with parsley.

PAUL NEWMAN
•
MARINATED STEAK

Ingredients
To serve 4 ✗✗✗

Metric/ Imperial		American
120 ml/4 fl oz	homemade vinaigrette	½ cup
2	garlic cloves	2
1	large onion	1
	salt and pepper	
1	large sirloin steak, about 4-cm/1½-in thick	1

Method
Place the dressing in a shallow glass dish. Peel and crush the garlic; peel and coarsely chop the onion. Add the onion and garlic to the dressing with seasoning to taste. Add the steak and turn to coat with the marinade. Cover and leave to marinate in the refrigerator for several hours, turning the steak occasionally.

Preheat the grill [broiler], or prepare a charcoal grill.

Drain the steak. Cook under the grill [broiler] or over charcoal until done to your taste. Slice and serve.

HENRY COOPER
•
STEAK AND KIDNEY PIE

Ingredients
To serve 6 ✖✖✖

Metric/ Imperial		American
1 kg/2¼ lb	lean chuck steak	2¼ lb
225 g/8 oz	kidney	½ lb
1	large onion	1
175 g/6 oz	mushrooms	1½ cups
2	garlic cloves (optional)	2
75 g/3 oz	flour	¾ cup
	salt and pepper	
3 tbsp	cooking oil	3 tbsp
75 g/3 oz	butter	6 tbsp
600 ml/1 pint	beef stock	2½ cups
300 ml/½ pint	red wine	1¼ cups
225 g/8 oz	puff pastry	½ lb
1	beaten egg to glaze	1

Method

Preheat the oven to 160°C/325°F/Gas 3.

Cut the steak into 2.5-cm/1-in cubes. Skin, core and chop the kidney. Peel and thinly slice the onion. Thinly slice the mushrooms. Peel and crush the garlic, if using.

Season the flour with salt and pepper and toss the steak and kidney in it. Shake off and reserve excess flour.

Heat the oil with 50 g/2 oz [¼ cup] of the butter in a frying pan. Add the steak and

kidney and fry over high heat until evenly browned. Stir in the remaining seasoned flour. Spoon the contents of the pan into a large casserole.

Heat the remaining butter in a clean pan and cook the onion until soft. Add the mushrooms and garlic and cook for 2–3 minutes longer. Stir in the stock and wine. Bring to the boil, then pour over the meat in the casserole.

Cover the casserole and cook in the oven for 1½–2 hours or until the meat is tender.

Remove the meat with a slotted spoon

and put it in a 2 l/3½-pint [2-quart] deep pie dish with a pie funnel in the centre. Reduce the casserole juices by fast boiling and pour over the meat. Leave to cool completely.

Roll out the pastry to 5-mm/¼-in thick and use to cover the pie dish. Brush with beaten egg. Increase the oven temperature to 230°C/450°F/Gas 8.

DAVE LEE TRAVIS
•
BEEF STROGANOFF

Ingredients
To serve 4 ✗ ✗

Metric/ Imperial		American
1	*medium onion*	1
225 g/8 oz	*button mushrooms*	*½ lb*
700 g/1½ lb	*fillet or sirloin steak*	*1½ lb*
25 g/1 oz	*butter*	*2 tbsp*
	salt and pepper	
1 tsp	*dijon mustard*	*1 tsp*
2 tbsp	*brandy*	*2 tbsp*
150 ml/¼ pint	*sour cream*	*½ cup*
2 tbsp	*chopped fresh parsley to garnish*	*2 tbsp*

Method
Peel and finely chop the onion. Slice the mushrooms. Cut the steak into thin strips.

Heat the butter in a large frying pan and cook the onion until soft and golden. Add the mushrooms and cook for a further 2 minutes. Add the steak strips and seasoning to taste, then stir in the mustard. Sauté briskly for 5 minutes or until the juices from the meat run pink.

Add the brandy and sour cream and stir to mix. Heat through gently; do not allow to boil or the cream will curdle. Taste and adjust the seasoning, then serve sprinkled with parsley.

ERNIE WISE
•
STEAK AND VEGETABLE CASSEROLE

Ingredients
To serve 4 ✖✖✖

Metric/ Imperial		American
450 g/1 lb	stewing or chuck steak	1 lb
2 tsp	flour	2 tsp
	salt and pepper	
2	medium onions	2
2	large carrots	2
1	sweet green pepper	1
2	celery stalks	2
2 tbsp	cooking oil	2 tbsp
100g/4 oz	button mushrooms	1 cup
1	bay leaf	1
450 ml/3/4 pint	beef stock	2 cups

Method
Preheat the oven to 160°C/325°F/Gas 3.

Cut the steak into bite-size pieces. Season the flour with salt and pepper and toss the meat in it. Peel and chop the onions. Peel and slice the carrots. Core, seed and slice the green pepper. Slice the celery. (Everything is very orderly in a Wise kitchen.)

Heat the oil in a flameproof casserole and fry the onions, carrots, green pepper and celery for about 10 minutes. Add the beef and continue frying until the pieces of meat are browned on all sides. Stir in the mushrooms, bay leaf, more seasoning and finally the stock. Bring to the boil.

Cover the casserole and transfer to the oven. Cook for 2 hours. It should then be a lovely casserole with tender meat. Ideal for a cold day, and marvellous for building up my short, fat, hairy legs.

GEOFFREY HOWE
•
HOTPOT

Ingredients
To serve 6–8 ✖✖✖

Metric/ Imperial		American
1.4 kg/3 lb	braising or chuck steak	3 lb
8	medium potatoes	8
3	medium onions	3
350 g/12 oz	mushrooms (optional)	3/4 lb
40 g/11/2 oz	butter	3 tbsp
15 g/1/2 oz	flour	2 tbsp
	salt and pepper	
450 ml/3/4 pint	beef stock	2 cups

Method
Preheat the oven to 160°C/325°F/Gas 3.

Cut the meat into 2.5-cm/1-in cubes. Peel the potatoes and cut into slices about 3-mm/ 1/8-in thick. Peel and slice the onions. If using mushrooms, slice them.

Use about half the butter to grease an iron or earthenware pot – preferably a tall round one. Put in a layer of potatoes, then a layer of meat, and onion and mushrooms. Continue layering the ingredients until all are used up, ending with potatoes. Sprinkle a little flour on each layer, and season the layers well. Pour over the stock and dot the top with the remaining butter.

Cover and cook in the oven for 2 hours. Uncover and cook for 30 minutes longer to brown the top. Serve very hot.

'Simple and delicious.' SIR GEOFFREY HOWE

NEIL KINNOCK
•
ROGHAN GOSH

Ingredients
To serve 4–6 ✗✗✗

Metric/ Imperial		American
900 g/2 lb	chuck steak (or lean boneless lamb)	2 lb
450 g/1 lb	onions	1 lb
2	garlic cloves	2
5-cm/2-in	piece of fresh root ginger	2-in
6 tbsp	cooking oil	6 tbsp
1 tsp	ground coriander	1 tsp
1/2 tsp	ground cinnamon	1/2 tsp
1 1/2 tsp	ground cumin	1 1/2 tsp
1 tsp	turmeric	1 tsp
1/4 tsp	chilli powder	1/4 tsp
225-g/8-oz	can of tomatoes	8-oz
6 tbsp	plain yogurt	6 tbsp

Method
Preheat the oven to 180°C/350°F/Gas 4.

Cut the beef or lamb into bite-size cubes. Peel and chop the onions. Peel and crush the garlic. Peel and grate or finely chop the ginger.

Heat the oil in a flameproof casserole and fry the onions and garlic until lightly browned. Add the meat cubes and brown on all sides. Remove the meat and onions with a slotted spoon.

Add the ginger, coriander, cinnamon, cumin, turmeric and chilli powder to the fat in the casserole and cook, stirring, for about 30 seconds, then stir in the tomatoes and yogurt. Return the meat and onions and stir to blend.

Transfer the casserole to the oven and cook for about 1 hour or until the meat is tender. Serve with plain boiled rice, poppadums, chapati or naan bread, mango chutney and a green vegetable salad.

TOMMY CANNON
•
BEEF CURRY

Ingredients
To serve 4 ✗✗✗

Metric/ Imperial		American
450 g/1 lb	braising or chuck steak	1 lb
1	onion	1
2 tbsp	cooking oil	2 tbsp
	salt and pepper	
1/2 tsp	ground ginger	1/2 tsp
1/2 tsp	chilli powder	1/2 tsp
4 tsp	curry powder	4 tsp
1 tbsp	tomato purée [paste]	1 tbsp
1	garlic clove	1
150 ml/1/4 pint	beef stock or water	1/2 cup
1 tsp	cornflour [cornstarch]	1 tsp
150 ml/1/4 pint	milk	1/2 cup

Method
Cut the steak into cubes. Peel and slice the onion. Heat the oil in a heavy saucepan and fry the steak and onion until the cubes of meat are browned on all sides. Add seasoning to taste, the ginger, chilli powder, curry powder and tomato purée [paste]. Peel and crush the garlic. Add to the pan and stir well. Add the stock or water. Bring to the boil, then cover and simmer until the meat is tender.

Dissolve the cornflour [cornstarch] in the milk and add to the pan, stirring well. Simmer for 20 minutes longer.

Serve with rice and poppadums.

PAM AYRES
•
COTSWOLD FANDANGO

Ingredients
To serve 4 ✗✗

Metric/ Imperial		American
1	onion	1
2 tbsp	cooking oil	2 tbsp
450 g/1 lb	minced [ground] beef	1 lb
1	egg	1
100 g/4 oz	flour	1 cup
300 ml/½ pint	milk	1½ cups
	salt	

Method
Preheat the oven to 220°C/425°F/Gas 7.

Take the onion – not from your neighbour's allotment – peel it and chop it up. Fling it into a frying pan in which you have heated the oil and fry until soft. Next, tip in a quantity of minced [ground] beef – whatever you've got. Fry the meat until it is browned. Pour off excess fattage, then place the beef and onion mixture in a small baking pan.

Combine the egg, flour, milk and salt to taste in a mixing bowl and beat well. Frighten it a bit. Pour this batter into the baking pan on top of the beef and onion. Bake until the top looks brown and inviting and done. Mind you, this can fool the unwary – it usually looks more done than it is so don't take it out until it is really brown and crispy on top. There you are.

Serve with gourmet vegetables such as canned peas or baked beans and mashed potato and a dazzling smile! Gravy is a good idea, or if it is overdone and a bit dry – a bucket of water!

'Much as I am anxious to give you my favourite recipe, I have to tell you that my ability to cook comes a long way down my list of attributes after charm, wit, egg-timer figure, Bo Derek lookalike, ace conker player etc. However, I am not one to flinch! This is one recipe that a half wit can do. I do it all the time!' PAM AYRES

56

JOHN HURT
•
DONNA'S TEXAS CHILLI

Ingredients
To serve 6–8 ✗ ✗

Metric/ Imperial		American
2	large onions	2
2	garlic cloves	2
1	sweet green pepper	1
3 tbsp	olive oil	3 tbsp
1.4 kg/3 lb	coarsely minced [ground] lean beef	3 lb
4 tbsp	chilli powder	1/4 cup
1 tbsp	ground cumin	1 tbsp
1/4 tsp	dried oregano	1/4 tsp
1	small bay leaf	1
2 400-g/14-oz	cans of tomatoes	2 16-oz
	salt	
3 tbsp	flour	2 tbsp
3 400-g/14-oz	cans of red kidney beans (optional)	3 16-oz

Method

Peel and chop the onions. Peel and crush the garlic. Core, seed and chop the green pepper. Heat the oil in a large pot and cook the onions, garlic and green pepper until lightly browned. Add the beef and cook until browned and crumbly.

Add the chilli powder, cumin, oregano, bay leaf, tomatoes and salt to taste. Stir well. Cover and cook gently for 1½ hours, stirring occasionally.

Dissolve the flour in a little water and stir into the chilli to thicken the liquid. If liked, add the drained kidney beans. Cook for a further 30 minutes.

PAUL SCOFIELD
•
KIDNEYS WITH MUSHROOMS AND YOGURT

Ingredients
To serve 4 ✗ ✗

Metric/ Imperial		American
700 g/1½ lb	ox [beef] kidney	1½ lb
2	medium onions	2
50 g/2 oz	butter	1/4 cup
175 g/6 oz	button mushrooms	1½ cups
2 tbsp	flour	1 tbsp
	salt	
pinch	cayenne pepper	pinch
300 ml/1/2 pint	plain yogurt	1¼ cups

Method

Cut out the centre core from the kidney and divide it. Blanch in boiling water for 3 minutes, then drain well. Slice the kidneys. Peel and thinly slice the onions.

Melt the butter in a deep frying pan and fry the kidney slices over a low heat for a few minutes. Remove with a slotted spoon and set aside. Add the onions to the pan and cook until soft. Stir in the mushrooms, and return the kidney slices to the pan. Sprinkle over the flour and stir well. Add salt and cayenne pepper to taste. Add the yogurt and cook gently, stirring, until thickened. Cover and cook for 20 minutes, stirring occasionally. Do not allow to boil or the yogurt will curdle.

Serve with plain boiled brown rice or noodles and a green salad.

ANTHONY QUAYLE
•
TRIPE CATALANE

Ingredients
To serve 4–6 ✖✖✖

Metric/ Imperial		American
900 g/2 lb	tripe	2 lb
1½	glasses of dry white wine	1½
3	onions	3
2	carrots	2
2	leeks	2
4	parsley sprigs	4
2	fresh thyme sprigs	2
1½	bay leaves	1½
4	tomatoes	4
1	garlic clove	1
50 g/2 oz	lard	¼ cup
½ tsp	grated nutmeg	½ tsp
3 tbsp	chopped fresh parsley	3 tbsp
1–2	fresh basil leaves	1–2
	fresh or dried marjoram	
	salt and pepper	

Method

Rinse the tripe well and put it into a large saucepan. Add ½ glass of wine. Peel and coarsely chop 2 onions and the carrots. Wash and chop the leeks. Add the prepared vegetables to the pan with the parsley sprigs, one thyme sprig, one bay leaf and cold water to cover. Bring to the boil and simmer for about 2 hours or until the tripe is very tender. Add more water during this time if necessary.

Drain the tripe and cut it into small pieces. Peel and finely chop the remaining onion. Peel and chop the tomatoes. Peel the garlic; crush half of it and finely chop the other half. Preheat the oven to 150°C/300°F/Gas 2.

Heat the lard in a shallow pan and add the tripe, finely chopped onion and tomatoes. Cook briskly for 3–4 minutes, then add the crushed garlic, a pinch of nutmeg, 2 tbsp of the parsley, the remaining ½ bay leaf, the basil, a little marjoram, the remaining wine, and seasoning to taste. Bring to the boil and cook over a moderate heat until the wine has reduced a little.

Transfer the pan to the oven and cook for 5 minutes. Sprinkle with the remaining chopped parsley and finely chopped garlic, and serve with rye bread and black olives.

VINCE HILL
•
OXTAIL CASSEROLE

Ingredients
To serve 4 ✖✖✖

Metric/ Imperial		American
1–2	oxtails	1–2
2	large onions	2
4 tbsp	flour for dredging	4 tbsp
4 tbsp	cooking oil	¼ cup
	salt and pepper	
2	garlic cloves	2
2	bay leaves	2
1 tsp	dried mixed herbs	1 tsp
150 ml/¼ pint	port	¾ cup
5	carrots	5
4	potatoes	4
2 tbsp	chopped fresh parsley to garnish	2 tbsp

Method

Have the butcher cut the oxtails into joints.

Peel and coarsely chop the onions. Coat the pieces of oxtail with flour. Heat the oil in a large heavy pot and cook the oxtail pieces until well browned all over – about 5 minutes at a good heat. Remove from the pan and set aside.

Add the onions to the pot and cook briskly, stirring, about 2–3 minutes. Return the oxtail pieces to the pot and add seasoning to taste. Peel and crush the garlic and add with the bay leaves and herbs. Just cover with water. Bring to the boil, then cover and simmer for 1 hour. Remove from the heat and leave to cool overnight.

The next day, remove the fat that will have solidified on the surface. Add the port and bring to the boil. Cover and simmer gently for 1½ hours.

Peel the carrots and cut into 2-cm/³⁄4-in thick pieces. Add to the pot and simmer for a further 30 minutes. Peel the potatoes and cut into eighths. Add and simmer for 30 minutes longer or until the potatoes are just tender. Stir occasionally.

Serve sprinkled with parsley.

BRIAN RIX
●
TRIPE AND ONIONS

Ingredients
To serve 4 ✗✗✗

Metric/ Imperial		American
450 g/1 lb	tripe	1 lb
150 ml/¼ pint	milk	½ cup
150 ml/¼ pint	water	½ cup
1	large onion	1
	salt and pepper	
15 g/½ oz	butter	1 tbsp
15 g/½ oz	flour	1 tbsp

Method

Rinse the tripe and cut it into pieces. Put it into a saucepan and add the milk and water. Peel and slice the onion. Add to the pan with seasoning to taste. Bring to the boil, then cover and simmer gently for 1 hour.

Melt the butter in another saucepan and add the flour. Cook gently, stirring, for 2–3 minutes. Gradually add the cooking liquid from the tripe, stirring well. Simmer, stirring, until thickened. Add the tripe to the sauce and simmer, covered, for a further 20 minutes.

BRIAN RIX

LAMB

JUDITH HANN
•
GRILLED BREAST OF LAMB

Ingredients
To serve 4 ✖✖✖

Metric/		
Imperial		American
1	large breast of lamb	1
1	onion	1
2	carrots	2
1 tsp	dried mixed herbs	1 tsp
	salt and pepper	
1	egg	1
4 tbsp	breadcrumbs	4 tbsp
4	lemon wedges	4
1 bunch	watercress	1 bunch
	tartare sauce to serve	

Method
Preheat the oven to 170°C/325°F/Gas 3.

Put the breast of lamb into a casserole. Peel and chop the onion and carrots. Add to the casserole with a pinch of herbs and salt and pepper to taste. Add water to cover. Cook in the oven for 2–3 hours or until the lamb is tender.

Remove the lamb from the casserole and allow it to cool. Skim any fat from the surface of the cooking liquid. If liked, dissolve a stock cube in it and serve it as soup.

Preheat the grill [broiler].

Remove the lamb meat from the bones, discarding all fat. Lightly beat the egg. Dip the pieces of meat in egg, then coat in breadcrumbs. Grill until crisp and golden brown on both sides.

Serve hot, with lemon wedges, watercress and tartare sauce.

DUGGIE BROWN
•
HONEY-GLAZED LAMB

Ingredients
To serve 6 ✖✖✖

Metric/		
Imperial		American
1	garlic clove (optional)	1
2-kg/4-lb	leg of lamb	4-lb
2 tbsp	crumbled dried rosemary	2 tbsp
	salt and pepper	
225 g/8 oz	thick honey	2/3 cup
150 ml/¼ pint	dry white wine or cider	½ cup
150 ml/¼ pint	water	½ cup
6	fresh rosemary sprigs to garnish	6

Method
Preheat the oven to 200°C/400°F/Gas 6.

If using the garlic, peel it and cut into slivers. Make incisions all over the leg of lamb with the tip of a sharp knife and insert the garlic slivers. Rub the lamb with the rosemary and seasoning to taste, then coat with the honey.

Place the lamb in a roasting pan and add the wine or cider and water to the pan. Roast for about 1¾ hours, basting with the liquid in the pan from time to time.

Serve garnished with fresh rosemary sprigs, if available, and make a gravy from the pan juices if liked.

DIANA RIGG

•

GIGOT DE MOUTON BOULANGÈRE

Ingredients

To serve 6–8 ✕ ✕ ✕

Metric/ Imperial		American
4–6	onions	4–6
6–8	potatoes	6–8
50 g/2 oz	butter	1/4 cup
	salt and pepper	
4	sliced tomatoes (optional)	4
1	leg of lamb	1

Method

Preheat the oven to 180°C/350°F/Gas 4.

Peel and thinly slice the onions and potatoes. Use about half the butter to grease a baking dish or roasting pan large enough to hold the leg of lamb. Make alternate layers of onion and potato in the dish, seasoning the layers, and ending with potato. Sliced tomatoes can be added too, if liked. Dot with the remaining butter. Add enough boiling water to the dish to come just below the top layer. Place the lamb on top.

Bake, allowing 20–25 minutes to each 450 g/1 lb of meat.

DAVID SHEPPARD
•
TRADITIONAL LANCASHIRE HOTPOT

Ingredients
To serve 4 ✖✖✖

Metric/ Imperial		American
4	lambs' kidneys	4
900 g/2 lb	potatoes	2 lb
350 g/12 oz	onions	¾ lb
	dripping or oil	
900 g/2 lb	best end and middle neck of lamb [blade or arm chops]	2 lb
1 tbsp	flour	1 tbsp
600 ml/1 pint	hot water	2½ cups
½ tsp	Worcestershire sauce	½ tsp
	salt and pepper	
1	bay leaf	1
2	fresh thyme sprigs	2
15 g/½ oz	butter	1 tbsp

Method

Preheat the oven to 160°C/325°F/Gas 3.

Core, skin and chop the kidneys. Peel the potatoes and cut into slices about 2-cm/¾-in thick. Peel and chop the onions.

Heat some dripping or oil in a large frying pan until it is very hot. Add a few pieces of lamb and fry until they are well browned on all sides. As the lamb is browned, transfer it to a wide casserole. Brown the pieces of kidney too, and tuck these in with the meat.

Next, fry the onions until they turn brown at the edges. Stir in the flour to soak up the juices, then gradually add the hot water, stirring well. Add the Worcestershire sauce and seasoning to taste. Bring to the boil. Pour this mixture over the meat in the casserole and add the bay leaf and thyme. Arrange the potato slices on top. Season the potatoes and add flecks of butter.

Cover tightly and cook in the oven for 1½ hours. Uncover and cook for a further 50 minutes. If you think the top is not browning enough, turn the heat in the oven right up during the last 15 minutes.

DAVID OWEN
•
KIDNEYS IN BUTTER AND MUSTARD SAUCE

Ingredients
To serve 2 ✖✖

Metric/ Imperial		American
6	lambs' kidneys	6
40 g/1½ oz	butter	3 tbsp
1 tbsp	finely chopped spring onion [scallion]	1 tbsp
5 tbsp	dry white wine	5 tbsp
1 tbsp	Dijon mustard	1 tbsp
	salt and pepper	

Method

Skin the kidneys and remove all white fat. Heat 25 g/1 oz [2 tbsp] of the butter in a deep frying pan and cook the kidneys for about 10 minutes or until browned all over but still pink in the centre. Remove the kidneys with a slotted spoon and set aside.

Add the spring onion [scallion] to the pan and cook for 1 minute. Add the wine and bring to the boil, scraping up all sediment from the bottom of the pan with a wooden spoon. Remove from the heat and stir in the mustard and seasoning to taste. Swirl in the remaining butter.

Cut the kidneys at a slight angle into slices about 5-mm/¼-in thick. Add to the pan. Reheat gently for 2–3 minutes, stirring to mix with the sauce. Add a sprinkle of parsley and serve with boiled rice.

VEAL

SEBASTIAN COE
•
SPAGHETTI VITELLO

Ingredients
To serve 4 ✗ ✗

Metric/ Imperial		American
700 g/1½ lb	veal steak, cut 2.5-cm/1-in thick	1½ lb
2 tbsp	flour	2 tbsp
½ tsp	dried oregano	½ tsp
	salt and pepper	
3	onions	3
4 tbsp	olive oil	¼ cup
150 ml/¼ pint	water	½ cup
75 g/3 oz	grated Parmesan cheese	¾ cup
450 g/1 lb	spaghetti	1 lb

Method

Preheat the oven to 180°C/350°F/Gas 4.

Cut the veal steak into four portions. Season the flour with the oregano and salt and pepper to taste and dip the veal in it to coat. Peel and slice the onions.

Heat the oil in a frying pan and fry the veal steaks until browned on both sides. Transfer them to a baking dish; reserve the oil in the frying pan. Add the onions and water to the baking dish. Cover and bake for about 1 hour.

Add about 50 g/2 oz [½ cup] of the cheese to the frying pan and stir over a low heat to make a sauce. Keep hot.

Cook the spaghetti in boiling salted water until just tender. Drain well.

Arrange the veal steaks in the centre of a serving dish and surround with the spaghetti. Cover with the cheese sauce and sprinkle the remaining cheese over the entire dish.

'To follow almost any meal, I will eat apple pie and fresh cream.' SEBASTIAN COE

CHRISTIAAN BARNARD
•
VEAL SCALOPPINE WITH TOMATOES

Ingredients
To serve 4 ✖✖

Metric/ Imperial		American
700 g/1½ lb	veal escalopes [scaloppine]	1½ lb
	flour for dredging	
225 g/8 oz	mushrooms	½ lb
1	garlic clove	1
2	medium tomatoes	2
15 g/½ oz	butter	1 tbsp
1 tbsp	olive oil	1 tbsp
2 tbsp	chopped fresh parsley	2 tbsp
2 tbsp	chopped fresh basil	2 tbsp
120 ml/4 fl oz	Marsala	½ cup
2 tbsp	grated Parmesan cheese	2 tbsp
	salt and pepper	

Method
Have the butcher pound the veal until thin
Preheat the oven to 160°C/325°F/Gas 3.

Cut the veal into 2.5-cm/1-in squares and dredge in flour. Shake off excess flour. Thinly slice the mushrooms. Peel and crush the garlic. Peel, seed and dice the tomatoes.

Heat the butter and oil in a frying pan and add the veal. Fry until browned on both sides. Tip the veal into a baking dish and add the mushrooms, garlic, tomatoes, herbs, Marsala, cheese and seasoning to taste. Stir to blend.

Cover and cook in the oven for about 45 minutes.

BASIL BRUSH
•
SALTIMBOCCA ALLA ROMANA

Ingredients
To serve 4 ✖✖

Metric/ Imperial		American
8 50-g/2-oz	veal escalopes [scaloppine]	8 2-oz
	salt	
8	fresh sage leaves	8
4 or 8	paper-thin slices of raw smoked ham [prosciutto crudo]	4 or 8
65 g/2½ oz	butter	5 tbsp
4 tbsp	dry white wine or Marsala	¼ cup

Method
Have the butcher beat the veal until thin.

Sprinkle each piece of veal with salt to taste. Lay a sage leaf on each, then cover with ½–1 slice of ham, trimmed to fit the veal neatly. Secure each little 'sandwich' with a wooden cocktail stick; these are never rolled up.

Heat 40 g/1½ oz [3 tbsp] of the butter in a large frying pan until foaming, then sauté the veal briskly on both sides for 6–8 minutes or until cooked through and golden. Transfer the veal to a warmed serving platter. Discard the cocktail sticks and keep hot.

Add the wine to the pan and bring to the boil, scraping the bottom of the pan with a wooden spoon to mix in the sediment. Swirl in the remaining butter. Pour this sauce over the veal and serve immediately.

CLEO LAINE
•
VEAL IN PAPRIKA SAUCE

Ingredients
To serve 4 ✗ ✗ ✗

Metric/ Imperial		American
700–900 g/ 1½–2 lb	lean boneless veal cut from the shoulder or leg	1½–2 lb
2 tbsp	flour	2 tbsp
	salt and pepper	
2	large onions	2
1	sweet green pepper	1
225 g/8 oz	tomatoes	½ lb
1	garlic clove	1
4 tbsp	cooking oil	¼ cup
1 tbsp	paprika	1 tbsp
150 ml/¼ pint	water	¾ cup
1 tbsp	tomato purée [paste]	1 tbsp
150–300 ml/ ¼–½ pint	sour cream	1 cup

Method

Cut the veal into 2.5-cm/1-in cubes. Season the flour with salt and pepper and toss the veal cubes in it to coat. Peel and chop the onions. Core, seed and chop the green pepper. Peel and chop the tomatoes. Peel and finely chop the garlic.

Heat the oil in a heavy large saucepan and cook the onions and green pepper gently until soft and pale gold. Add the veal cubes, increase the heat and fry until golden brown on all sides.

Add the tomatoes, garlic, paprika, water and tomato purée [paste] and stir well. Bring to the boil, then cover and simmer gently for 1½–2 hours or until the meat is tender. Stir occasionally.

Blend in the sour cream and heat through without boiling. Serve with plain boiled rice or noodles.

DAVID PUTTNAM
•
OSSOBUCO MILANESE

Ingredients
To serve 4 ✗✗✗

Metric/ Imperial		American
900 g/2 lb	shin of veal [veal shanks]	2 lb
50 g/2 oz	butter	1/4 cup
150 ml/1/4 pint	dry white wine	1/2 cup
350 g/12 oz	tomatoes	3/4 lb
150 ml/1/4 pint	veal or chicken stock	1/2 cup
	salt and pepper	
	handful of fresh parsley	
1	garlic clove	1
1/2	lemon	1/2

Method

If using shin [shank] from a full-grown calf, allow 1.8 kg/4 lb. Have the butcher saw the veal shin [shank] into pieces 5-cm/2-in thick.

Heat the butter in a heavy casserole and brown the slices of veal on both sides. Once browned, arrange the slices in the pan so that they are upright, in order to keep the marrow in the bone during cooking. Pour the wine over the veal and cook for 10 minutes.

Meanwhile, peel and chop the tomatoes. Add them to the pan and let them reduce for a few minutes, then add the stock and seasoning to taste. Cover and cook for 1½–2 hours.

Just before serving, chop the parsley. Peel and finely chop the garlic. Finely grate the rind from the lemon half. Mix together the parsley, garlic and lemon rind. The Milanese call this mixture *gremolata*, and it is an essential part of the traditional *ossobuco*.

Sprinkle the *gremolata* on top of the veal before serving.

PORK

RUSSELL HARTY
•
SAVOURY PORK CHOPS

Ingredients
To serve 4 ✗✗

Metric/ Imperial		American
1	onion	1
1 tbsp	flour	1 tbsp
	salt and pepper	
4	pork chops	4
25 g/1 oz	butter	2 tbsp
120 ml/4 fl oz	medium sherry	1/2 cup
175 ml/6 fl oz	chicken stock	3/4 cup
2 tbsp	light French mustard	2 tbsp

Method

Peel and thinly slice the onion. Season the flour with salt and pepper and use to coat the chops lightly.

Heat the butter in a large frying pan and cook the onion until soft. Remove the onion with a slotted spoon. Add the chops to the pan and fry briskly until browned.

Return the onion to the pan and add the sherry and stock. Cover and simmer for 30 minutes or until the chops are cooked.

Transfer the chops to a warmed serving dish and keep hot. Add the mustard to the sauce in the pan and stir well. Taste and adjust the seasoning. Pour the sauce over the chops and serve.

GEOFFREY HUGHES
•
PORK CHOPS WITH SAGE AND APPLE

Ingredients
To serve 4 ✖✖

Metric/ Imperial		American
4 tbsp	dry white breadcrumbs	1/4 cup
2 1/2 tbsp	finely chopped fresh sage or	2 1/2 tbsp
2 tsp	dried sage	2 tsp
	salt and pepper	
1	small egg	1
4	pork chops	4
25 g/1 oz	butter	2 tbsp
2 tbsp	cooking oil	2 tbsp
1	medium onion	1
1	large cooking apple	1

Method

Mix together the breadcrumbs, sage and seasoning to taste. Lightly beat the egg in a shallow dish. Trim all fat from the chops, then dip them in the beaten egg and coat with the crumb mixture. Press the crumb mixture onto the chops to help it adhere.

Heat half the butter and oil in a large frying pan. Add the chops and brown briskly on both sides, then reduce the heat and cover the pan. Cook for about 20 minutes longer, turning once, or until the chops are cooked through.

Meanwhile, peel and slice the onion into rings. Peel and core the apple and cut into rings. Heat the remaining butter and oil in another frying pan and cook the onion and apple rings until tender.

Serve the chops with the onion and apple rings spooned over.

RON PICKERING

•

BARBECUED SPARERIBS

Ingredients
To serve 2–4 ✗ ✗ ✗

Metric/ Imperial		American
700 g/1½ lb	pork spareribs	1½ lb
1 tsp	dry mustard	1 tsp
2 tbsp	brown sugar	2 tbsp
2 tbsp	tomato ketchup	2 tbsp
2 tbsp	vinegar	2 tbsp
2 tbsp	water	2 tbsp
1 tbsp	Worcestershire sauce	1 tbsp
	salt and pepper	
Savoury rice		
1	onion	1
1 tbsp	cooking oil	1 tbsp
225 g/8 oz	long-grain rice	1 cup
600 ml/1 pint	chicken stock	2½ cups
2	bacon slices	2
100 g/4 oz	sliced mushrooms	1 cup
225 g/8 oz	cooked peas	1½ cups

Method

Preheat the oven to 180°C/350°F/Gas 4.

Cut the spareribs into 1- or 2-rib pieces and arrange them in a baking pan. Cook in the oven for 45 minutes to 1 hour or until lightly browned. Pour off all the fat from the pan.

Mix together the mustard, sugar, ketchup, vinegar, water, Worcestershire sauce and seasoning to taste. Pour this sauce over the ribs, turning them so that they are evenly coated. Cover and return to the oven. Cook for a further 1–1½ hours, basting frequently with the sauce in the pan. The ribs will absorb the sauce while they cook and extra sauce should be made if necessary.

Meanwhile, prepare the rice. Peel and finely chop the onion. Heat the oil in a small flameproof casserole and cook the onion until soft. Add the rice and cook, stirring, for 1 minute, then stir in the stock. Add seasoning to taste. Bring to the boil. Cover the casserole and transfer to the oven. Bake for 20 minutes or until the rice is tender and all the stock has been absorbed.

While the rice is cooking, chop the bacon, discarding any rind, and fry with the mushrooms until browned. Add the bacon, mushrooms and peas to the rice before serving. Small pieces of cooked chicken and hard-boiled egg may be added to the rice too.

Serve the spareribs with the savoury rice.

GARETH THOMAS
•
WELSH SPARERIBS

Ingredients
To serve 4 ✗✗

Metric/ Imperial		American
1	medium leek	1
4	tomatoes	4
4	pork sparerib chops [blade chops]	4
½ tsp	grated nutmeg	½ tsp
	salt and pepper	
100 g/4 oz	cottage cheese	½ cup

Method

Preheat the oven to 180°C/350°F/Gas 4.

Thoroughly wash the leek, then slice it thinly crossways. Slice the tomatoes.

Arrange the chops in a baking pan in one layer. Sprinkle with a little nutmeg and seasoning to taste. Spread the cottage cheese over the chops, then add the leek. Cover with the tomatoes.

Cover the pan and cook in the oven for 30–45 minutes. Serve with new potatoes and a green salad.

ROY HUDD
•
SAUSAGE AND TOMATO PIE

Ingredients
To serve 4 ✗✗

Metric/ Imperial		American
1	small onion	1
2	large tomatoes	2
25 g/1 oz	butter	2 tbsp
450 g/1 lb	pork sausages [links]	1 lb
	salt and pepper	
150 ml/¼ pint	beef stock	½ cup
450 g/1 lb	hot mashed potatoes	2 cups

Method

Preheat the oven to 220°C/425°F/Gas 7.

Peel and slice the onion and tomatoes. Heat half the butter in a frying pan and fry the onion until soft. Remove with a slotted spoon and set aside.

Add the sausages to the pan and fry until well browned on all sides. Alternatively, the sausages may be cooked under the grill [broiler]. Remove the skin from the sausages and cut them in half lengthways. Lay half the sausage halves in a baking dish and cover with the onion and tomatoes. Add seasoning to taste, then cover with the remaining sausage halves. Add the stock to the dish and cover with a thick layer of mashed potato. Fork up the potatoes and dot with the remaining butter. Bake until browned.

BRIAN MURPHY
•
BANGERS AND MASH

Ingredients
To serve 1 ✖✖

Metric/ Imperial		American
2	large potatoes	2
1	onion	1
4	sausages	4
1	small bottle of brown ale [dark beer]	1
1 tsp	butter	1 tsp
1–2 tbsp	milk	1–2 tbsp
1 tsp	flour	1 tsp
	salt and pepper	

Method

Peel the potatoes and cook in boiling water until tender.

Meanwhile, peel and slice the onion. Fry the sausages with the onion in a frying pan. (If the sausages do not give off enough fat, add a little oil to the pan.) When the sausages are browned on all sides, add the ale [beer]. Cook for a further 10 minutes, stirring occasionally.

Drain the potatoes and return them to the pan. Add the butter and milk and mash until smooth.

Pile the mashed potatoes on a warmed place, scatter over the onion slices and stick the sausages upright in the mash. Keep hot.

Dissolve the flour in a little cold water, then add to the liquid in the pan. Cook, stirring, until thickened. Add salt and pepper to taste, then pour this over the sausages and mash.

PETER DAVISON
•
HAM STEAK HAWAII

Ingredients
To serve 4–6 ✖✖

Metric/ Imperial		American
75 g/3 oz	light brown sugar	1/2 cup
50 g/2 oz	butter	1/4 cup
4 tbsp	red wine vinegar	1/4 cup
700 g/1½ lb	smoked ham or gammon steak, cut 1–2 cm/½–¾ in thick	1½ lb
4	firm bananas	4
1	bunch of watercress to garnish	1

Method

Heat the sugar, butter and vinegar in a frying pan, stirring to dissolve the sugar and melt the butter. Add the ham steak to the pan and cook for about 5 minutes on each side or until cooked through. Remove the steak to a warmed serving dish and keep hot.

Peel the bananas and cut them into pieces about 4-cm/1½-in long. Add to the syrup in the frying pan and cook for about 5 minutes, stirring constantly.

Arrange the bananas around the ham steak and spoon over the syrup. Garnish with watercress and serve hot.

WILLIAM WHITELAW
•
CUMBERLAND SAUCE

Ingredients
To serve 4 ✗

Metric/		
Imperial		American
2	oranges	2
4 tbsp	redcurrant jelly	¼ cup
1½ tsp	Dijon mustard	1½ tsp
	salt and pepper	
7–8 tbsp	medium tawny port	7–8 tbsp

Method

Thinly pare the rind from the oranges. Cut the rind into fine shreds and blanch in a pan of boiling water for 5 minutes. Drain well.

Put the orange rind in a heatproof mixing bowl, or the top of a double boiler, and add the jelly, mustard and seasoning to taste. Place over a pan of hot water and heat, stirring constantly, until smooth. Add the port and cook, stirring, for a further 5 minutes.

Serve the sauce cold, with ham or game.

JEAN ALEXANDER
•
ROAST HAM

Ingredients
To serve many ✗ ✗ ✗

Metric/		
Imperial		American
1	ham, or piece of uncooked gammon	1
2 tbsp	prepared mustard	2 tbsp
225 g/8 oz	brown sugar	½ lb
20	whole cloves	20

Method

Calculate the cooking time for the ham: 20 minutes to each 450 g/1 lb plus an extra 20 minutes.

Place the ham in a large saucepan and add cold water to cover. Bring to the boil and simmer for one-third of the cooking time.

Preheat the oven to 190°C/375°F/Gas 5.

Drain the ham and allow to cool slightly. Strip off the rind and score the fat in a criss-cross pattern. Spread with mustard and press on a thick layer of brown sugar. Stud with cloves.

Place the ham in a lightly oiled roasting pan and roast for the remainder of the cooking time.

POULTRY

AND

GAME
MAIN
COURSES

DELIA SMITH
•
CURRIED CREAM CHICKEN

Ingredients
To serve 4 ✗✗

Metric/ Imperial		American
450 g/1 lb	cooked chicken meat	1 lb
1	large onion	1
2	celery stalks	2
1	large sweet green pepper	1
2 tbsp	cooking oil	2 tbsp
1 tsp	ground ginger	1 tsp
1–1½ tbsp	hot curry powder	1–1½ tbsp
1 tsp	turmeric	1 tsp
1	garlic clove	1
1½ tbsp	flour	1 tbsp
600 ml/1 pint	chicken stock	2½ cups
	salt and pepper	
2 tbsp	double [heavy] cream	2 tbsp

Method

Cut the chicken meat into 2.5-cm/1-in cubes, discarding any skin and bone. Set the chicken aside. Peel and roughly chop the onion. Chop the celery. Core, seed and chop the green pepper.

Heat the oil in a heavy saucepan and add the onion. Cook for about 5 minutes or until softened, then add the celery and green pepper. Cook for a further 5 minutes. Add the chicken pieces and mix them with the vegetables. Next stir in the ginger, curry powder and turmeric. Peel and crush the garlic and add to the pan. Stir in the flour to soak up all the juices.

Gradually add the chicken stock, stirring well after each addition. Add seasoning to taste. Cover and simmer for 20–25 minutes or until the vegetables are just tender.

Stir in the cream and serve hot, with rice and mango chutney.

73

PATRICK MOORE
•
CURRY À LA SELSEY

Ingredients
To serve 4–6 ✗✗

Metric/ Imperial		American
6	large apples	6
3	onions	3
2 tbsp	cooking oil	2 tbsp
225 g/8 oz	leftover vegetables such as potatoes, beans, carrots, etc.	2 cups
225 g/8 oz	leftover cooked chicken or roasted meat	2 cups
450 ml/¾ pint	chicken stock or	2 cups
300-g/11½-oz	can of tomato soup	12-oz
50 g/2 oz	sultanas [golden raisins]	½ cup
25 g/1 oz	raisins	¼ cup
3	bananas	3
2 tbsp	desiccated [shredded] coconut (optional)	2 tbsp
2 tsp	curry powder	2 tsp
½ tsp	chilli powder	½ tsp
	chopped fresh chillies [hot chili peppers]	

Method

Peel and chop the apples and onions. Heat the oil in a frying pan and add the apples and onions. Cook until soft.

Meanwhile, cut the leftover vegetables and meat into reasonably small pieces. Put them into a large saucepan and add the stock or soup. Heat, then tip in the apples and onions. Add plenty of sultanas [golden raisins], raisins, the chopped bananas and coconut if you like. Heat. Stir in curry powder, chilli powder and chillies to taste. My usual method is to make the main curry mild; separate half of it and heat up with further curry powder, etc. Separate half of this and make it really hot – so that everyone knows which type of heat they are choosing.

Make rice in the usual way. Serve the curry hot, with the rice and plenty of chutney, etc.

'This is probably the amateur's way of making curry, but I do it – and it works.' PATRICK MOORE

JIMMY HILL
●
CURRIED CHICKEN WITH PEACHES

Ingredients
To serve 4 ✖ ✖

Metric/ Imperial		American
2 tbsp	ground almonds or desiccated [shredded] coconut	2 tbsp
150 ml/¼ pint	boiling water	¾ cup
1.75-kg/ 3½-lb	chicken	3½-lb
1	medium onion	1
1	garlic clove	1
3 tbsp	olive oil or	3 tbsp
40 g/1½ oz	butter	3 tbsp
1–1½ tbsp	curry powder	1–1½ tbsp
½ oz/15 g	flour	1 tbsp
450 ml/¾ pint	chicken stock, preferably made from the giblets	2 cups
1 tbsp	redcurrant jelly	1 tbsp
3–4 tbsp	double [heavy] cream	3–4 tbsp
1 tsp	arrowroot (optional)	1 tsp
2	ripe peaches	2

Method
Combine the ground almonds or coconut and boiling water in a mixing bowl. Set aside to infuse for 1 hour, then strain the liquid and set aside.

Cut the chicken into serving pieces. Peel and finely chop the onion. Peel and crush the garlic.

Heat 2 tbsp of the oil or butter in a flameproof casserole. Add the chicken pieces and brown on all sides. Remove the chicken from the pot and set aside.

Add the remaining oil or butter to the casserole. Add the onion and cook gently until it is just turning colour. Stir in the curry powder and cook for 2–3 minutes, then stir in the flour and cook for a further 1 minute. Gradually stir in the stock. Add the garlic and simmer for 20 minutes.

Return the chicken to the casserole. Cover tightly and continue cooking for about 45 minutes or until very tender.

Remove the chicken pieces and strain the sauce into a clean pan. Add the almond or coconut milk and the redcurrant jelly to the sauce and simmer for 2–3 minutes. Stir in the cream. If necessary, thicken the sauce with the arrowroot dissolved in a little water.

Peel, stone [pit] and slice the peaches. Add them to the sauce with the chicken. Heat through gently, and serve hot with rice.

75

LEON BRITTAN
•
BREAST OF CHICKEN CORIANDER

Ingredients
To serve 4 ✗✗✗

Metric/ Imperial		American
450 g/1 lb	boneless chicken breasts	1 lb
2 tsp	coriander seeds	2 tsp
2.5-cm/1-in	piece of fresh root ginger *or*	1-in
½ tsp	ground ginger	½ tsp
2	garlic cloves	2
2 tbsp	tomato purée [paste]	2 tbsp
1	lemon	1
3 tbsp	cooking oil	3 tbsp
	salt and pepper	
1	small head of celery	1
150 ml/¼ pint	single [light] cream	½ cup
100 g/4 oz	cashew nuts	1 cup

Method

Remove the skin from the chicken breasts and cut across into fairly thin slices. Grind the coriander seeds in a pestle and mortar or spice grinder or with a rolling pin. If using fresh ginger, peel it and chop it finely with the peeled garlic. Combine the coriander, ginger, garlic, tomato purée [paste], juice of the lemon, 2 tbsp of the oil and seasoning to taste in a mixing bowl. Add the chicken strips and stir to coat. Trim and slice the celery and add to the bowl. Cover and marinate in the refrigerator for at least 8 hours or overnight.

Transfer the chicken mixture to a fairly shallow casserole dish and let stand at room temperature for 30 minutes.

Preheat the oven to 180°C/350°F/Gas 4.

Cover the casserole and cook in the oven for 50–60 minutes. Stir in the cream and bake for a further 5–10 minutes, just to heat through.

Meanwhile, heat the remaining oil and fry the cashew nuts until golden.

Scatter the nuts over the chicken mixture and serve hot.

'This is really very good.' LEON BRITTAN

BILL OWEN
•
CHICKEN PAPRIKA

Ingredients
To serve 4 ✗✗

Metric/ Imperial		American
1	large onion	1
25 g/1 oz	butter	2 tbsp
1 tbsp	medium sweet paprika	1 tbsp
4	chicken pieces, with giblets if available	4
1 tbsp	tomato purée [paste] *or*	1 tbsp
2	ripe tomatoes	2
1	sweet green pepper	1

Method

Peel and slice the onion. Heat the butter in a frying pan and add the onion. Cook until transparent but not browned. Sprinkle over the paprika and stir in well. Add the chicken pieces and giblets and fry until lightly browned on all sides.

Add the tomato purée [paste]. If using fresh tomatoes, chop them before adding. Core, seed and slice the green pepper and add. Cover and cook gently until the chicken is tender, stirring from time to time.

Serve hot with sour cream, new potatoes or rice, and a salad.

FIONA FULLERTON
•
PÂTÉ-STUFFED CHICKEN BREASTS IN MARSALA CREAM

Ingredients
To serve 6 ✖✖

Metric/Imperial		American
	handful dried porcini or cèpes	
2–3 tbsp	tepid water	2–3 tbsp
100 g/4 oz	chicken liver pâté	1/4 lb
6	large chicken breasts, boned	6
	salt and pepper	
2	shallots	2
100 g/4 oz	button mushrooms	1/4 lb
25 g/1 oz	butter	2 tbsp
1 tbsp	sunflower oil	1 tbsp
6 tbsp	Marsala	6 tbsp
300 ml/1/2 pint	double [heavy] cream	1 cup

Method

Soak the *porcini* or *cèpes* in the tepid water for 1 hour or so. Lift the mushrooms out of the liquid and squeeze them over the bowl to extract excess liquid. Reserve the liquid. Chop the mushrooms and mix with the pâté.

Cut a pocket in each chicken breast, extending the whole length of each breast. Divide the mushrooms and pâté mixture between the pockets in the chicken breasts, and season with salt and pepper to taste.

Peel and finely chop the shallots. Thinly slice the button mushrooms.

Heat the butter and oil in a shallow pan large enough to take the chicken breasts in one layer. Add the shallots and sliced mushrooms and cook until just wilted. Remove the vegetables with a slotted spoon and set aside.

Add the chicken breasts to the pan and cook until golden on both sides. Add the Marsala and reserved mushroom soaking liquid and continue cooking until the liquid has reduced to one-third.

Reduce the heat to low and stir in the cream. Return the shallots and sliced mushrooms to the pan, reserving a few mushroom slices for the garnish. Cook gently until the sauce thickens and the chicken breasts are cooked through. Taste and adjust the seasoning.

Serve hot, garnished with the reserved mushroom slices.

TREVOR NUNN
•
CHICKEN FILLETS IN HERB MUSTARD SAUCE

Ingredients
To serve 4 ✖

Metric/Imperial		American
4–8	chicken fillets (skinless, boneless breasts)	4–8
25 g/1 oz	butter	2 tbsp
2 tbsp	olive oil	2 tbsp
300 ml/1/2 pint	single [light] cream	1 1/4 cups
1 tbsp	herb mustard	1 tbsp
	salt and pepper	

Method

Trim any fat or cartilage from the chicken fillets. Heat the butter with the oil in a large frying pan and add the chicken. Cook, turning as necessary, until golden brown and tender. Add the cream, plenty of herb mustard to taste, and seasoning to taste. Heat, stirring, until the sauce thickens and just starts to bubble, then serve immediately.

GWYNETH POWELL
•
CORONATION CHICKEN

Ingredients
To serve 6–8 ✖ ✖ ✖

Metric/ Imperial		American
2	young roasting chickens	2
1	carrot	1
1	bouquet garni	1
3–4	black peppercorns	3–4
	salt	
1	glass of white wine	1
Sauce		
1	small onion	1
1 tbsp	vegetable oil	1 tbsp
1 tbsp	curry powder	1 tbsp
1 tsp	tomato purée [paste]	1 tsp
1	wineglass of red wine	1
1	wineglass of water	1
1	bay leaf	1
1–2	lemon slices	1–2
	lemon juice	
1 tsp	sugar	1 tsp
	salt and pepper	
450 ml/³/4 pint	mayonnaise	2 cups
1–2 tbsp	apricot purée	1–2 tbsp
4 tbsp	double [heavy] cream	¹/4 cup

Method

Place the chickens in a large saucepan or flameproof casserole. Add the carrot, bouquet garni, peppercorns and salt to taste. Pour in the wine and add enough water just to cover the chicken. Bring to the boil, then poach gently for about 40 minutes or until the chickens are cooked through and tender. Leave to cool in the stock.

When the chicken is cold, drain it (reserving the strained stock for soup). Discard the skin and remove the chicken meat from the bones, keeping the meat in large pieces.

To make the sauce, peel and finely chop the onion. Heat the oil in a saucepan, add the onion and cook until softened. Sprinkle over the curry powder and cook for 1–2 minutes longer, stirring well. Add the tomato purée [paste], wine, water and bay leaf and stir. Bring to the boil, then add the lemon slices, a good squeeze of lemon juice, a little sugar to taste, and salt and pepper to taste. Simmer for 5–10 minutes. Strain and allow to cool.

When cold, gradually whisk the curry liquid into the mayonnaise with the apricot purée. Taste and add more lemon juice, salt and pepper, if desired. Whip the cream until thick and fold into the sauce.

Add the sauce to the chicken meat and fold together gently. Arrange on a serving plate and serve chilled.

ROBERT LINDSAY
•
A STUFFING FOR CHICKEN

Ingredients
To serve 4 ✖

Metric/ Imperial		American
1	large onion	1
2 tbsp	chopped seedless grapes	2 tbsp
2 tbsp	chopped nuts	2 tbsp
2 tbsp	grated apple	2 tbsp
100 g/4 oz	fresh breadcrumbs	1 cup
1 tsp	fresh or dried sage	1 tsp
1	large egg	1

Method

Peel and very finely chop or grate the onion. Mix with the grapes, nuts, apple, breadcrumbs and sage. Bind with the beaten egg. Place the mixture in the chicken. Roast as usual.

MICHAEL CRAWFORD
•
CHICKEN AND LEEK PIE

Ingredients
To serve 6 ✗ ✗ ✗

Metric/ Imperial		American
2.5-kg/5-lb	chicken	5-lb
2	medium onions	2
2	celery stalks	2
1	bouquet garni	1
	salt and pepper	
1 kg/2½ lb	leeks	2½ lb
1 tbsp	chopped fresh parsley	1 tbsp
100 g/4 oz	cooked ham	¼ lb
1 tsp	sugar	1 tsp
175 g/6 oz	puff or rough puff pastry, thawed if frozen	6 oz
	milk to glaze	

Method
Place the chicken in a large saucepan. Peel and halve the onions and add to the pan. Quarter the celery and add, with the bouquet garni and 2 tsp salt. Cover with water. Bring to the boil, skimming off any scum that rises to the surface. Reduce the heat, partly cover the pan and simmer for 1–1½ hours or until the chicken is tender.

Transfer the chicken to a carving board. Strain the stock into a measuring jug. Return 450 ml/¾ pint [2 cups] of the stock to the pan. Thoroughly wash and slice the leeks and add to the pan. Simmer until just tender.

Preheat the oven to 200°C/400°F/Gas 6.

Remove the chicken meat from the carcass and discard all skin and bones. Cut the meat into bite-size pieces and put into a deep pie dish. Pour in the leeks and stock. Add the parsley. Chop the ham and add it with the sugar.

Roll out the pastry and use to cover the top of the dish. Make a slit in the centre of the pastry lid to allow the steam to escape. Brush the pastry with a little milk, then bake until the pastry is well risen and golden brown. Serve hot.

FRED HOUSEGO
●
POLLO CACCIATORA

Ingredients
To serve 4 ✗ ✗

Metric/ Imperial		American
1	medium onion	1
175 g/6 oz	mushrooms	1½ cups
6	tomatoes	6
1	garlic clove	1
2-kg/4-lb	chicken	4-lb
25 g/1 oz	butter	2 tbsp
2 tbsp	olive oil	2 tbsp
1	bay leaf	1
250 ml/8 fl oz	dry white wine	1 cup
120 ml/4 fl oz	chicken stock	½ cup
	salt and pepper	
15 g/½ oz	flour	1 tbsp

Method

Peel and finely chop the onion. Chop the mushrooms. Peel and chop the tomatoes. Peel and crush the garlic. Cut the chicken into eight pieces.

Heat half the butter with the oil in a heavy casserole over moderate heat. Add the onion and cook until softened. Add the mushrooms and cook for a further 2–3 minutes. Remove the vegetables with a slotted spoon and set aside.

Add the chicken pieces to the casserole and brown lightly on all sides. Return the onion and mushrooms to the pot and add the tomatoes, garlic, bay leaf, wine, stock and seasoning to taste. Bring to the boil and simmer gently for about 45 minutes or until the chicken is tender.

Remove the chicken with a slotted spoon and keep it hot. Increase the heat under the casserole and boil to reduce the liquid by about one-quarter. Mash together the flour and remaining butter to make a paste and add to the liquid, in small pieces, stirring. When the liquid has thickened, taste and adjust the seasoning, and discard the bay leaf.

Serve the chicken on bed of mashed potato, and pour the sauce over the top.

MARGARET THATCHER

•

COLD CHICKEN VÉRONIQUE

Ingredients
To serve 4–6 ✗✗✗

Metric/Imperial		American
1	young chicken	1
2	egg yolks	2
300 ml/½ pint	cream	1¼ cups
1	glass of sherry	1
	finely grated lemon rind to garnish	
Rice salad		
275 g/10 oz	long-grain rice	1½ cups
2 tbsp	olive oil	2 tbsp
1 tbsp	tarragon vinegar	1 tbsp
	salt and pepper	
50 g/2 oz	stoned [pitted] black olives	½ cup
50 g/2 oz	chopped celery	½ cup
50 g/2 oz	peeled and sliced tomatoes	½ cup
50 g/2 oz	chopped sweet green and red peppers	½ cup

Method

Poach the chicken in water or stock to cover until it is tender. Allow to cool in the liquid, then drain well. (Reserve the cooking liquid for another dish.) Cut the chicken into serving pieces and arrange on a serving dish.

Lightly beat the egg yolks with the cream and sherry in a mixing bowl or the top of a double boiler. Place over a pan of hot water and stir until slightly thickened. Do not boil. Pour this sauce over the chicken and sprinkle with grated lemon rind. The sauce will gradually thicken as the dish cools.

To make the rice salad, cook the rice in boiling salted water until tender. Drain well, if necessary, and while still warm, mix in some olive oil, vinegar and seasoning to taste. When cool, add the remaining ingredients and fold together gently.

Serve the chicken with the rice salad.

BARBARA CARTLAND

•

CHICKEN WITH ORANGE SURPRISE

Ingredients
To serve 4 ✘ ✘ ✘

Metric/ Imperial		American
1 tsp	ground ginger	1 tsp
	salt and pepper	
1.5-kg/3-lb	chicken	3-lb
1	onion	1
½	orange	½
25 g/1 oz	butter	2 tbsp
1 tbsp	cornflour [cornstarch]	1 tbsp
150 ml/¼ pint	orange juice	½ cup
150 ml/¼ pint	cider	½ cup
2 tbsp	golden syrup [light corn syrup]	2 tbsp
8	orange segments to garnish	8

Method

Preheat the oven to 180°C/350°F/Gas 4.

Mix together the ginger and seasoning and rub into the skin of the chicken. Place the chicken in a roasting pan and roast for 1¼–1½ hours or until tender.

About 20 minutes before the chicken is ready, prepare the sauce. Peel and thinly slice the onion. Thinly pare the rind from the ½ orange and cut the rind into fine shreds. Heat the butter in a small pan and cook the onion and orange rind until the onion is soft and translucent.

Dissolve the cornflour [cornstarch] in a little of the orange juice. Add to the remaining juice. Add to the onion with the cider and bring to the boil, stirring. Stir in the syrup. Simmer until thickened. Add seasoning to taste.

Remove the chicken from the oven and cut it into serving pieces. Arrange them on a serving plate. Spoon over the hot sauce and garnish with orange segments. Serve hot.

'This is one of the favourite dishes I serve in my home and which I invented with my chef, Nigel Gordon.'
BARBARA CARTLAND

WILLY BRANDT
•
CHICKEN IN RED WINE

Ingredients
To serve 4 ✗✗✗

Metric/ Imperial		American
50 g/2 oz	butter	1/4 cup
1.75-kg/ 3½-lb	chicken	3½-lb
50 g/2 oz	lean bacon	2 oz
8	button [pearl] onions	8
3 tbsp	brandy	3 tbsp
450 ml/3/4 pint	red wine (Burgundy-type)	2 cups
150 ml/1/4 pint	chicken stock	1/2 cup
1	garlic clove	1
1	bay leaf	1
4	parsley sprigs	4
4	thyme sprigs	4
	salt and pepper	
100 g/4 oz	button mushrooms	1 cup
25 g/1 oz	flour	2 tbsp

Method
Heat half the butter in a flameproof casserole and add the chicken. Brown it on all sides, turning with the aid of two large spoons. Remove the chicken from the pot.

Chop the bacon. Peel the onions. Add the bacon and onions to the casserole and fry until the onions are golden brown. Return the chicken to the pot. Warm the brandy, pour it over the chicken and set alight. When the flames have died down, add the wine and chicken stock. Peel and crush the garlic and add with the bay leaf, a few parsley and thyme sprigs and seasoning to taste. Bring to the boil. Cover and simmer for 45 minutes.

Add the mushrooms and simmer for a further 15 minutes or until the chicken is tender.

Transfer the chicken to a warmed serving dish. Arrange the onions and mushrooms around the chicken. Keep hot.

Remove and discard the herbs from the cooking liquid. Mix the remaining butter with the flour to make a paste. Add in small pieces to the liquid, stirring, and simmer until thickened. Taste and adjust the seasoning, then pour this sauce over.

WILLIE CARSON
•
ROAST GROUSE WITH BRANDY CREAM

Ingredients
To serve 4 ✗✗

Metric/ Imperial		American
50 g/2 oz	butter	1/4 cup
2	young grouse	2
150 ml/1/4 pint	brandy	1/2 cup
300 ml/1/2 pint	double [heavy] cream	1 cup
	salt and pepper	

Method
Preheat the oven to 170°C/325°F/Gas 3.

Melt the butter in a frying pan, add the grouse and brown them on all sides. Transfer the grouse to a roasting pan and pour over the melted butter. Roast for 40 minutes or until the grouse are done; test with a skewer – the juices that run out should be clear.

Transfer the grouse to a warmed serving platter and keep hot. Place the roasting tin on top of the stove and add the brandy. Bring to the boil, stirring to mix in the sediments in the pan. Add the cream and boil until reduced and saucelike. Add salt and pepper to taste.

Serve the grouse with the brandy cream sauce.

'I like all food, but my favourite is grouse.' WILLIE CARSON

TONY HART
•
ROAST DUCK IN ORANGE SAUCE

Ingredients
To serve 3–4 ✗✗✗

Metric/ Imperial		American
1	*orange*	1
25 g/1 oz	*butter*	*2 tbsp*
	salt and pepper	
1	*duck*	1
150 ml/¼ pint	*chicken stock*	*½ cup*
1	*glass of red wine*	1
	Sauce	
1	*small carrot*	1
1	*small onion*	1
1	*small celery stalk*	1
50 g/2 oz	*butter*	*¼ cup*
1 tbsp	*flour*	*1 tbsp*
600 ml/1 pint	*beef stock*	*2½ cups*
1 tsp	*tomato purée [paste]*	*1 tsp*
1	*bouquet garni*	1
25 g/1 oz	*mushroom peelings*	*¼ cup*
2 tbsp	*redcurrant jelly*	*2 tbsp*
	Garnish	
2	*oranges*	2
	lettuce	
	watercress	

Method
Preheat the oven to 190°C/375°F/Gas 5.

Thinly pare the rind from the orange; set the orange aside. Put the orange rind, half the butter and seasoning to taste inside the duck. Smear the remaining butter over the skin of the duck. Place it in a roasting pan with the stock. Roast for about 1½ hours, basting occasionally with the stock.

Meanwhile, make the sauce. Peel and dice the carrot and onion. Dice the celery. Melt the butter in a saucepan and add the diced vegetables. Cook on a low heat until the vegetables are golden brown. Stir in the flour and cook until golden. Gradually add the stock, stirring well, then add the tomato purée [paste], bouquet garni and mushroom peelings. Bring to the boil and leave to simmer for 25 minutes.

Skim any fat from the sauce and strain it into a clean saucepan. Set aside.

When the duck is cooked, transfer it to a warmed serving platter and keep hot. Skim any fat from the juices in the roasting pan. Add the red wine and the juice from the orange and bring to the boil, stirring well to mix in the sediments in the pan. Strain into the sauce. Add the redcurrant jelly and heat, stirring. Taste and adjust the seasoning.

For the garnish, peel the oranges, removing any pith and membrane, and slice them. Arrange around the duck with lettuce and watercress. Serve with the sauce.

JOHN ARLOTT
•
CASSOULET

Ingredients
To serve 4–6 ✗✗✗

Metric/ Imperial		American
450 g/1 lb	*dried white beans, preferably flageolets*	*1 lb*
2	*onions*	2
100 g/4 oz	*bacon*	*¼ lb*
2	*garlic cloves*	2
1	*tomato*	1
600 ml/1 pint	*beef stock*	*2½ cups*
1	*bouquet garni*	1
	salt and pepper	
4–6	*pieces of cooked goose*	4–6
2 tbsp	*goose dripping*	*2 tbsp*
450 g/1 lb	*sausages, ideally saucisses de Toulouse*	*1 lb*
50 g/2 oz	*fresh breadcrumbs*	*1 cup*

Method

Soak the beans in water to cover overnight. The next day, drain the beans, place them in a saucepan and cover with fresh cold water. Bring to the boil and simmer for about 1½ hours. Drain again.

Peel and slice the onions. Cut the bacon into squares, discarding any rind. Peel and crush one garlic clove. Peel the tomato.

Cook the onions and bacon together gently until the onions are softened. Add the crushed garlic, tomato, stock, bouquet garni and seasoning. Bring to the boil and allow to simmer for 20 minutes.

Preheat the oven to 150°C/300°F/Gas 2.

Halve the remaining garlic clove and rub the cut sides over the inside of an earthenware pot. Put the pieces of goose and the goose dripping on the bottom. Cover with the sausages and add the bacon mixture, then add the beans. Bring slowly to the boil on top of the stove, then spread a layer of breadcrumbs over the top and transfer to the oven. Bake for 1 hour.

Variation: Duck or pork can be used instead of goose, but the goose dripping gives the dish a distinctive richness and flavour.

BRIAN CLOUGH
•
FAMILY TURKEY PIE

Ingredients
To serve 4 ✗✗

Metric/ Imperial		American
75 g/3 oz	fatty bacon	3 oz
1	medium onion	1
25 g/1 oz	butter or margarine	2 tbsp
25 g/1 oz	flour	2 tbsp
150 ml/¼ pint	turkey or chicken stock	¾ cup
150 ml/¼ pint	milk	½ cup
225 g/8 oz	cooked turkey meat	½ lb
1 tbsp	lemon juice	1 tbsp
½ tsp	grated nutmeg	½ tsp
	salt and pepper	
225 g/8 oz	puff or shortcrust [pie] pastry	8 oz
1	beaten egg to glaze	1

Method

Chop the bacon. Peel and chop the onion. Cook the bacon and onion in a small pan until the bacon is crisp and the onion is lightly browned. Drain and set aside.

Melt the butter in a saucepan and add the flour. Cook, stirring, for 1 minute. Gradually stir in the stock and milk and bring to the boil, stirring. Simmer until thickened. Add the bacon and onion. Chop the turkey and add with the lemon juice, a pinch of nutmeg, and seasoning to taste. Cover and allow to cool.

Preheat the oven to 200°C/400°F/Gas 6.

Pour the turkey mixture into a deep pie dish. Cover with the pastry and brush with beaten egg. Bake for about 30 minutes or until golden brown.

EGG, PASTA
AND
VEGETABLE MEALS

EGGS

JEREMY IRONS
•
CHAMP

Ingredients
To serve 4 ✖ ✖

Metric/ Imperial		American
700 g/1½ lb	potatoes	1½ lb
10	spring onions [scallions] or	10
2	leeks	2
200 ml/⅓ pint	milk	1 cup
50 g/2 oz	butter	¼ cup
	salt and pepper	
6	eggs	6
2 tbsp	grated Parmesan cheese	2 tbsp
2 tbsp	chopped fresh parsley to garnish	2 tbsp

Method

Peel and quarter the potatoes. Cook them in boiling water until tender. Drain.

Meanwhile, chop the spring onions [scallions]. If using leeks, wash them thoroughly and cut into thin slices. Cook the onions or leeks in the milk until tender. Drain, reserving the milk, and set aside.

Drain the potatoes and return them to the pan. Add half the butter and seasoning to taste and mash until smooth. Mix in the onions or leeks, then add sufficient hot milk to make a fluffy mixture. Keep hot.

Lightly beat the eggs with the Parmesan and seasoning to taste. Melt the remaining butter in a heavy saucepan and cook the egg mixture over a low heat until creamy and just scrambled. Stir frequently.

Spoon the potato mixture around the edge of a heated serving dish to form an even border. Tip the eggs into the centre and sprinkle with parsley. Serve immediately.

87

STRATFORD JOHNS

•

SPINACH, CHEESE AND EGG GRILL

Ingredients
To serve 1 ✗

Metric/ Imperial		American
4	spinach leaves	4
50 g/2 oz	cottage cheese	1/4 cup
2	eggs	2
1 tbsp	grated Parmesan cheese	1 tbsp
	salt and pepper	

Method

Wash the spinach leaves and remove any coarse stalks. Drain. Cook in a covered saucepan until wilted. There should be enough water clinging to the leaves for cooking. Drain well, pressing out all excess water. Chop the spinach.

Preheat the grill [broiler].

Place the spinach in an individual gratin dish or other small flameproof serving dish. Spread over a layer of cottage cheese and make two hollows in it with a large spoon. Break the eggs into the hollows. Sprinkle with Parmesan cheese and seasoning to taste.

Grill [broil] until the eggs are just set and the top is golden brown.

'This is very good for fat people. Guess who?'
STRATFORD JOHNS

PENELOPE KEITH

•

GOUGÈRE

Ingredients
To serve 4 ✗✗

Metric/ Imperial		American
100 g/4 oz	butter	1/2 cup
	salt	
450 ml/3/4 pint	milk	2 1/2 cups
225 g/8 oz	flour	2 cups
6	eggs	6
175 g/6 oz	Gruyère cheese	6 oz
1–2 tbsp	grated Gruyère cheese	1–2 tbsp

Method

Preheat the oven to 200°C/400°F/Gas 6.

Put the butter in a heavy saucepan with a pinch of salt and half the milk. Bring to the boil, stirring to help melt the butter. Stir the remaining milk with the flour to make a smooth paste and pour the boiling milk and butter mixture onto it, stirring all the time. Add the eggs, one at a time, beating well. The mixture should be smooth, thick and creamy. Cut the 175 g/6 oz Gruyère into small pieces and add to the mixture.

Pour the mixture into a deep buttered pie dish and sprinkle over the grated cheese. Bake for 30 minutes or until puffed and golden brown. Serve hot or cold.

ROBERT RUNCIE
•
EGGS WITH SHRIMPS

Ingredients
To serve 4 ✗

Metric/ Imperial		American
150 ml/¼ pint	hot béchamel sauce	¾ cup
4	hard-boiled eggs	4
1½ tbsp	chopped fresh parsley	1½ tbsp
100 g/4 oz	peeled cooked shrimps, thawed if frozen	¼ lb
15 g/½ oz	butter	1 tbsp
pinch	cayenne pepper	pinch
	salt and pepper	
25 g/1 oz	grated cheese	¼ cup

Method
Preheat the grill [broiler].

Warm the sauce in a saucepan. Finely chop the eggs and add to the pan with the parsley, shrimps, butter and seasoning to taste. Heat through briefly.

Spoon the mixture into individual flame-proof dishes and sprinkle with the cheese. Brown under the grill [broiler].

'I think my favourite dish is well-cooked pork sausages which have burst a little. Since I keep excellent pigs as a hobby, I can have these from time to time; but I have to watch that I don't put on too much weight because there are some people who think that a fat Archbishop is an offence to the Gospel!' ROBERT RUNCIE

LESTER PIGGOTT
•
CHEESE SOUFFLÉ

Ingredients
To serve 4 ✗✗

Metric/ Imperial		American
40 g/1½ oz	butter	3 tbsp
40 g/1½ oz	flour	3 tbsp
300 ml/½ pint	milk	1¼ cups
½ tsp	dry mustard	½ tsp
	salt and pepper	
75 g/3 oz	grated cheese	¾ cup
3	egg yolks	3
4	egg whites	4

Method

Preheat the oven to 180°C/350°F/Gas 4.

Melt the butter in a saucepan and stir in the flour. Cook, stirring, for 1–2 minutes. Gradually stir in the milk and cook until thickened. Add mustard and seasoning to taste. Stir in the cheese until melted.

Remove the pan from the heat. Add the egg yolks and mix in well. Beat the egg whites until stiff and fold into the mixture. Spoon into a soufflé dish.

Bake for 35 minutes or until risen and golden brown. Serve immediately.

PAT PHOENIX
•
EGG AND TUNA PICKUPS

Ingredients
To serve 4–6 ✖✖

Metric/ Imperial		American
225 g/8 oz	flour	2 cups
	salt and pepper	
50 g/2 oz	butter	1/4 cup
50 g/2 oz	lard	1/4 cup
3–4 tbsp	water	1/3 cup
2	hard-boiled eggs	2
90-g/3 1/2-oz	can of tuna fish	3 1/2-oz
1 tbsp	tomato ketchup	1 tbsp
1 tbsp	lemon juice	1 tbsp

Method

Place the flour, a pinch of salt, the butter and lard in the bowl of a food processor. Blend until the mixture resembles breadcrumbs. Add the water through the feeder tube and process to a firm dough. Alternatively, sift the flour and salt into a bowl and rub in the fats until the mixture resembles breadcrumbs. Mix in the water and knead briefly into a firm dough. Chill.

Preheat the oven to 200°C/400°F/Gas 6.

Combine the eggs, drained tuna fish, ketchup, lemon juice and seasoning to taste in the food processor and process just until the ingredients are mixed.

Roll out the dough into a 30 × 23 cm/ 12 × 9 in oblong. Cut into 12 76.5-cm/3-in squares.

Place a little of the tuna mixture in the centre of each square. Dampen the edges and fold over to form triangles. Press the edges to seal. Arrange on a baking sheet and bake for 25 minutes or until golden brown.

PASTA

MICHAEL FISH
•
PASTA CARBONARA

Ingredients
To serve 4–6 ⏳

Metric/ Imperial		American
500 g/1 lb	bacon	1 lb
750 g/1½ lb	mushrooms	1½ lb
500 g/1 lb	pasta shells	1 lb
25 g/1 oz	butter	2 tbsp
4 tbsp	grated Parmesan cheese	¼ cup
300 ml/½ pint	single [light] cream	1 cup
	salt and pepper	

Method
Remove any rind from the bacon, then dice it. Slice the mushrooms.

Cook the pasta shells in boiling water until just tender.

Meanwhile, fry the bacon in a frying pan until crisp and golden brown. At the same time, melt the butter in another pan and cook the mushrooms until wilted.

Drain excess fat from the bacon, then add the mushrooms, cheese, cream and salt and pepper to taste. Stir well. Heat through gently but do not allow to boil.

Drain the pasta and serve with the sauce.

CLAIRE RAYNER
•
VEGETABLE LASAGNE

Ingredients
To serve 4 ✖✖✖

Metric/ Imperial		American
1	onion	1
2 tbsp	cooking oil	2 tbsp
400-g/14-oz	can of tomatoes	16-oz
½ tsp	dried oregano or basil	½ tsp
	salt and pepper	
450 g/1 lb	selection of cooked vegetables, such as carrots, celery, courgettes [zucchini], aubergine [eggplant], etc.	1 lb
225 g/½ lb	mozzarella cheese	½ lb
50 g/2 oz	fresh brown breadcrumbs	1 cup
25 g/1 oz	bran (optional)	¼ cup

Method
Peel and finely chop the onion. Heat the oil in a saucepan and cook the onion until soft. Add the tomatoes. Add herbs and seasoning to taste. Cook until the sauce is thick and rich.

Preheat the oven to 180°C/350°F/Gas 4.

Arrange a layer of vegetables in a baking dish and spoon over a layer of the tomato sauce. Add a layer of thinly sliced mozzarella cheese. Repeat the layers until all the ingredients are used up, finishing with a layer of cheese. Strew the top with a mixture of breadcrumbs, oregano or basil to taste and bran, if liked.

Bake for about 45 minutes or until the top is crisp.

PAMELA STEPHENSON
•
PAMELA'S PASTA WITH VEGETABLE SURPRISES

Ingredients
To serve as many as required ✗ ✗

Metric/ Imperial		American
100 g/4 oz	wholewheat pasta	1 cup
75–100 g/ 3–4 oz	chopped mushrooms	1 cup
25 g/1 oz	margarine	2 tbsp
1 tsp	chopped fresh oregano or other favourite herb	1 tsp
1 tbsp	miso	1 tbsp
Vegetable surprise 1		
225 g/¹/₂ lb	Jerusalem artichokes	¹/₂ lb
225 g/¹/₂ lb	carrots	¹/₂ lb
1	onion	1
450 g/1 lb	broccoli	1 lb
Vegetable surprise 2		
1	aubergine [eggplant]	1
225 g/¹/₂ lb	tomatoes	¹/₂ lb
	cooking oil	
25 g/1 oz	grated Parmesan cheese	¹/₄ cup
50 g/2 oz	lentil sprouts	1 cup

Method

To make vegetable surprise 1, peel the Jerusalem artichokes, carrots and onion. Cut these vegetables, and the broccoli, into bite-size pieces. Place the vegetables in a saucepan and add enough water to come halfway up the vegetables. Cover tightly and simmer until tender but still crisp. The water should be absorbed, but keep checking the saucepan doesn't go dry and add a little more water if the vegetables are not cooked.

For vegetable surprise 2, chop the aubergine [eggplant] and tomatoes into small pieces, and fry in just enough oil to cover the bottom of a pan. Sprinkle liberally with cheese, cover and cook over a low heat, stirring occasionally, until tender. Toss with lentil sprouts before serving.

For the pasta, cook it in boiling water until just tender. Meanwhile, cook the mushrooms in margarine. Drain the pasta and add to the mushrooms. Add the herb and allow to heat through on a very low flame for a couple of minutes. Remove from the heat and mix in a spoonful of miso dissolved in 3 tbsp warm water.

Serve the pasta accompanied by the two vegetable dishes.

SUSANNAH YORK
•
PASTA COSA NOSTRA

Ingredients
To serve 5–6 ✖

Metric/ Imperial		American
1	onion (optional)	1
2–3	garlic cloves	2–3
450 g/1 lb	tomatoes or	1 lb
2 400-g/14-oz	cans of tomatoes	2 16-oz
1	sweet green pepper	1
1/2	sweet red pepper	1/2
225 g/8 oz	mushrooms	1/2 lb
3 tbsp	olive oil	3 tbsp
2–3	bay leaves	2–3
pinch	dried oregano	pinch
1 tbsp	tomato purée [paste]	1 tbsp
	salt and pepper	
100 g/4 oz	black olives	3/4 cup
1/2	glass of wine (optional)	1/2
450 g/1 lb	fresh pasta	1 lb
	grated Parmesan cheese to serve	

Method

Peel and finely chop the onion, if using. Peel and crush the garlic. If using fresh tomatoes, chop them. Core, seed and chop the peppers. Slice the mushrooms.

Heat all but 1 tsp oil in a saucepan and cook the onion and garlic until soft. Add the tomatoes, peppers, mushrooms, bay leaves, oregano, tomato purée [paste], seasoning and a few black olives if you have them. If you have half a glass of wine handy, add that too. Simmer, stirring occasionally, until a good sauce consistency.

Drop the pasta into a large saucepan of boiling salted water with 1 tsp oil. Cook until just tender. Drain well.

Spoon the sauce over the pasta and serve with freshly grated cheese.

JANE ASHER
•
PASTA, CHEESE AND CORN CASSEROLE

Ingredients
To serve 4 ✖✖

Metric/ Imperial		American
100 g/4 oz	pasta shapes	1/4 lb
50 g/2 oz	butter	1/4 cup
50 g/2 oz	flour	1/4 cup
600 ml/1 pint	milk	2 1/2 cups
175–225 g/ 6–8 oz	grated cheese	1 1/2–2 cups
200-g/7-oz	can of corn	7-oz
3	tomatoes	3

Method

Preheat the oven to 200°C/400°F/Gas 6.

Cook the pasta in boiling water for about 10 minutes or until just tender.

Meanwhile, melt the butter in a saucepan and add the flour. Cook, stirring, for 1–2 minutes, then pour in the milk (yes, all at once!). Stir briskly until the sauce thickens and the lumps are all blended in. Remove from the heat and stir in most of the cheese.

Drain the pasta. Drain the corn. Add the pasta and corn to the cheese sauce and fold together. Pour into a greased shallow baking dish. Sprinkle over the rest of the cheese. Slice the tomatoes and arrange over the top.

Bake for about 15 minutes.

DESMOND LYNAM
•
MACARONI CHEESE DE LUXE

Ingredients
To serve 4 ✗✗

Metric/ Imperial		American
100 g/4 oz	macaroni	4 oz
4	bacon slices	4
2	small tomatoes	2
25 g/1 oz	butter	2 tbsp
25 g/1 oz	flour	2 tbsp
300 ml/½ pint	milk	1 cup
175 g/6 oz	grated Cheddar cheese	1½ cups
1 tsp	prepared English mustard	1 tsp
	salt and pepper	
	toast triangles	

Method
Cook the macaroni in boiling water until just tender. Meanwhile, cut any rind from the bacon slices. Cut each slice in half crossways, then roll up the bacon pieces and thread them onto a skewer. Set aside. Halve the tomatoes and thread onto a skewer so the cut sides are all facing upwards. Set aside.

Preheat the grill [broiler].

Melt the butter in a saucepan and stir in the flour. Cook, stirring, for 2 minutes, then gradually stir in the milk. Bring to the boil, still stirring, and simmer until thickened. Add all but about 2 tbsp of the cheese, the mustard and salt and pepper to taste.

Drain the macaroni well and fold into the cheese sauce. Spoon into a greased flame-proof dish and sprinkle the reserved cheese over the top. Place the dish under the grill [broiler], along with the skewers of bacon and tomato, and cook. Garnish the macaroni cheese with the bacon rolls, tomato halves and toast triangles and serve.

CHRISTOPHER REEVE
•
SPAGHETTINI ALLA VONGOLE

Ingredients
To serve 4 ✗✗

Metric/ Imperial		American
12	clams	12
1½	garlic cloves	1½
3 tbsp	olive oil	3 tbsp
1 tsp	chopped anchovy fillets or anchovy paste	1 tsp
1½ tbsp	chopped parsley	1½ tbsp
400-g/14-oz	can of tomatoes	16-oz
	salt and pepper	
450 g/1 lb	spaghettini	1 lb

Method
Scrub the clams and rinse thoroughly. Place them in a saucepan, cover and cook over high heat until the shells open. (Discard any clams that remain closed.) Detach the clams from the shells and rinse off any sand on the meat by dipping them briefly, one at a time, in their own juice. Unless the clams are exceptioally small, cut them into two or more pieces and set aside. Strain the clam juices through a sieve lined with kitchen paper towels and set aside.

Peel and finely chop the garlic. Heat the oil in a saucepan and cook the garlic over moderate heat until lightly coloured. Add the chopped anchovies or paste and parsley. Chop the tomatoes with their juice and add to the pan with the strained clam juices. Add seasoning to taste. Stir well, then simmer for 25 minutes. Remove from the heat.

When the sauce is nearly ready, cook the spaghettini. Stir the clams into the sauce and add to the pasta and mix together well. Serve immediately, without grated cheese.

VEGETABLES

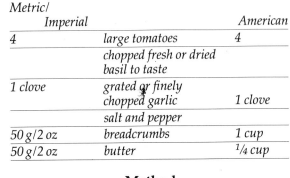

JILLY COOPER
•
BAKED TOMATOES

Ingredients
To serve 4 ⧗

Metric/ Imperial		American
4	*large tomatoes*	4
	chopped fresh or dried basil to taste	
1 clove	*grated or finely chopped garlic*	*1 clove*
	salt and pepper	
50 g/2 oz	*breadcrumbs*	*1 cup*
50 g/2 oz	*butter*	*¼ cup*

Method

Preheat the oven to 180°C/350°F/Gas 4.

Cut the tomatoes in half and arrange them in a baking dish. Sprinkle the cut surfaces with basil, garlic and a little seasoning to taste, then cover with breadcrumbs and top with bits of chopped butter. Bake for about 20 minutes.

BOB WILSON
•
COURGETTES MAISON

Ingredients
To serve 4 ✗✗

Metric/ Imperial		American
8	small courgettes [zucchini]	8
4	tomatoes	4
1	shallot	1
50 g/2 oz	butter	1/4 cup
1 tsp	paprika	1 tsp
	salt and pepper	
225 g/8 oz	cooked peeled prawns [shrimp]	1/2 lb
25 g/1 oz	flour	2 tbsp
300 ml/1/2 pint	milk	1 cup
50 g/2 oz	grated Parmesan cheese	1/2 cup

Method

Trim the ends from the courgettes [zucchini]. Cook them whole in boiling water for 5 minutes, then drain well and refresh in cold water. Leave to cool.

Peel, seed and chop the tomatoes. Peel and finely chop the shallot.

Preheat the oven to 220°C/425°F/Gas 7.

Cut a slice lengthways from each courgettes [zucchini], and scoop out the flesh with the point of a teaspoon. Keep the shells intact. Chop the flesh.

Melt half the butter in a frying pan, add the shallot and cook until softened. Add the chopped courgette [zucchini] flesh, tomatoes, paprika and salt and pepper to taste. Cook briskly for 2–3 minutes. Stir in the prawns [shrimp]. Remove from the heat and set aside.

Melt the remaining butter in a saucepan and stir in the flour. Cook, stirring, for 2 minutes, then gradually stir in the milk. Bring to the boil, stirring, and simmer until thickened. Add salt and pepper to taste.

Arrange the courgette [zucchini] shells in a greased baking dish, in one layer. Fill them with the vegetable and prawn mixture and spoon over the sauce. Sprinkle with the cheese. Bake for 10–12 minutes or until the top is browned. Serve hot.

NORMAN WISDOM
•
STUFFED BAKED POTATOES

Ingredients
To serve 4 ✗✗✗

Metric/ Imperial		American
4	baking potatoes	4
1	onion	1
25 g/1 oz	butter	2 tbsp
100 g/4 oz	grated cheese	1 cup
	salt and pepper	

Method

Preheat the oven to 190°C/375°F/Gas 5.

Scrub the potatoes and prick them in several places with the point of a sharp knife. Bake for 1–1½ hours or until tender.

Peel and finely chop the onion.

Heat the butter in a saucepan and cook the onion until softened. Remove from the heat.

Cut a slice off a long side of each potato and scoop out the inside into a mixing bowl. Add the onion and butter in which it was cooked. Add all but about 2 tbsp of the cheese. Mix well together. Add seasoning to taste. Pile the mixture back into the potato skins and sprinkle the tops with the reserved cheese.

Bake for a further 5–10 minutes or until the cheese topping has melted and is golden brown.

YEHUDI MENUHIN

●

STUFFED AUBERGINES [EGGPLANTS]

Ingredients
To serve 4 ✖✖

Metric/ Imperial		American
4	large aubergines [eggplants]	4
	salt and pepper	
2	onions	2
2	garlic cloves	2
100–150 g/ 4–6 oz	mushrooms	1–1¹⁄₂ cups
15 g/¹⁄₂ oz	butter	1 tbsp
4	large ripe tomatoes	4
1 tbsp	tomato purée [paste]	1 tbsp
2 tbsp	chopped mixed fresh herbs (parsley, marjoram, thyme, oregano)	2 tbsp
300 ml/¹⁄₂ pint	stock	1¹⁄₄ cups
5–6	anchovy fillets	5–6
50 g/2 oz	black olives	¹⁄₃ cup
75 g/3 oz	fresh brown breadcrumbs	1¹⁄₂ cups
75 g/3 oz	grated Gruyère cheese	³⁄₄ cup
	olive oil	

Method

Cut the aubergines [eggplants] in half lengthways and scoop out the pulp into a mixing bowl, leaving the shells intact. Sprinkle the inside of the shells with salt and leave to drain for about 30 minutes.

Meanwhile, chop the aubergine [eggplant] pulp. Peel and finely chop the onions. Peel and crush the garlic. Thinly slice the mushrooms. Heat the butter in a pan and cook the onions, aubergine [eggplant] pulp and mushrooms gently until very soft.

Preheat the oven to 180°C/350°F/Gas 4.

Peel, seed and chop the tomatoes. Add to the pan with the tomato purée [paste], the herbs, garlic and stock and stir well. Chop the anchovies and add them with some stoned [pitted] black olives. Mix together the breadcrumbs and cheese and add the tomato mixture. Stir well.

Rinse the aubergine [eggplant] shells and pat them dry carefully. Paint the skin of each shell with olive oil and pile the tomato mixture into each. Arrange in a baking dish and cover. Bake until the shells have softened and the filling is cooked through. Serve hot.

BARBARA DICKSON
•
VEGETABLE TARTS

Ingredients
To serve 4 ✗✗

Metric/ Imperial		American
150 g/6 oz	wholemeal [whole wheat] flour	1½ cups
75 g/3 oz	polyunsaturated margarine	6 tbsp
50 g/2 oz	grated Cheddar cheese	¼ cup
Filling		
1 tbsp	polyunsaturated margarine	1 tbsp
1 tbsp	wholemeal [whole wheat] flour	1 tbsp
300 ml/½ pint	milk	1¼ cups
	salt and pepper	
1	egg yolk	1
1 tbsp	lemon juice	1 tbsp
8	cooked cauliflower florets	8
100 g/4 oz	cooked diced carrots	1 cup
100 g/4 oz	cooked peas	1 cup

Method
Preheat the oven to 220°C/425°F/Gas 7.

Put the flour in a bowl and rub in the margarine until the mixture resembles breadcrumbs. Add just enough water to bind to a dough. Roll out the dough and sprinkle over the cheese. Form into a ball and roll out again. Use to line greased tartlet tins.

Bake blind until set and golden brown, about 20–25 minutes.

Meanwhile, make the filling. Melt the margarine in a saucepan and stir in the flour. Cook, stirring, for 1 minute, then gradually stir in the milk. Simmer, stirring, until thickened. Add seasoning to taste. Lightly beat the egg yolk and add to the sauce. Cook over a low heat without boiling for about 1 minute, still stirring. Add the lemon juice, then fold in the cooked vegetables. In addition you can add any other leftover cooked vegetable, cut up small, or 1 chopped cooked onion. Heat through gently.

Remove the tartlet cases from the tins and fill with the vegetable mixture. If liked, brown the tops under a preheated grill [broiler]. Serve piping hot, or cold.

VICTORIA WOOD
•
VEGETABLE CASSEROLE

Ingredients
To serve 4 ✗✗✗

Metric/ Imperial		American
2	parsnips	2
2	potatoes	2
3	onions	3
½	cauliflower	½
175 g/6 oz	grated Cheddar cheese	1½ cups
	salt and pepper	
300 ml/½ pint	milk	1¼ cups
2 tbsp	Marmite (yeast extract)	2 tbsp

Method
Preheat the oven to 180°C/350°F/Gas 4.

Peel and slice the parsnips, potatoes and onions. Separate the cauliflower into small florets. Layer the vegetables in a baking dish, sprinkling the layers with 100 g/4 oz [1 cup] of the cheese and seasoning to taste.

Heat the milk and stir in the yeast extract. Pour over the vegetables in the dish and sprinkle the top with the remaining cheese. Cover and bake for 1½ hours.

SUPPER
DISHES

TERRY WOGAN
●
CHIP BUTTIE

Ingredients
To serve 1 ⧗

Metric/ Imperial		American
2	slices of fresh white bread	2
15 g/½ oz	butter	1 tbs
8–10	hot chips [French fries]	8–10
	salt and pepper	

Method
Spread the bread liberally with butter and fill with sizzling hot freshly fried chips. Season to taste and eat!

LES DAWSON
•
RISOTTO

Ingredients
To serve 4 ✗✗

Metric/ Imperial		American
2	onions	2
1	garlic clove	1
6 tbsp	olive oil	6 tbsp
400 g/14 oz	long-grain rice	2 cups
1 l/1¾ pints	good chicken stock	1 quart
4 tbsp	grated cheese	4 tbsp
	salt and pepper	

Method

Peel and finely chop the onions. Peel and finely chop the garlic. Heat the oil in a large saucepan and cook the onions and garlic until soft. Add the rice and stir until coated with oil. Add the stock and bring to the boil. Stir once and cook until the stock has been absorbed and the rice is soft and creamy but not sticky. Stir in the cheese and seasoning to taste.

The thing about risotto is that it is versatile – you can add anything you like to it, even the mother-in-law!

SELINA SCOTT
•
BACON AND EGG PIE

Ingredients
To serve 4 ✗✗

Metric/ Imperial		American
225 g/8 oz	frozen puff pastry	½ lb
225 g/8 oz	lean bacon	½ lb
3	large eggs	3
1 tsp	dry mustard	1 tsp
	salt and pepper	

Method

Allow the pastry to thaw. Preheat the oven to 200°C/400°F/Gas 6.

Roll out half the pastry and use to line a 20-cm/8-in pie or quiche pan. Line with foil and bake blind for 10 minutes.

Meanwhile, cut the bacon into small squares, discarding any rind. Lightly beat the eggs with the mustard and seasoning to taste.

Remove the foil lining from the pastry case. Scatter the bacon over the bottom and pour over the egg mixture. Roll out the remaining pastry and use to cover the pie. Pinch the edges together to seal.

Bake for 25 minutes or until the pastry lid is golden brown. Allow to cool before serving.

WINDSOR DAVIES
•
CIG MOCH GYDA BARA LAWR (LAVER BREAD)

Ingredients
To serve as many as liked ✕

Welsh bacon	
fresh laver bread	
pepper	
vinegar	
fresh bread and butter	

Method
Fry the bacon until crisp and keep it hot. Heat the laver bread thoroughly in the bacon fat, then sprinkle it with pepper and vinegar to taste.

Eat the laver bread with the bacon and fresh bread and butter.

BERNARD MILES
•
BACON ROLL PUDDING

Ingredients
To serve 6–8 ✕✕✕

Metric/Imperial		American
500 g/1 lb	fat bacon [ham]	1 lb
6	cooking apples	6
1	onion	1
900 g/2 lb	flour	8 cups

Method
Boil a pound of fat bacon for half an hour, and then cut it up into thin slices. Peel six apples and one onion, and cut them in slices. Make two pounds of flour into a stiff dough, roll it out thin; first lay the slices of bacon out all over this, and then upon the slices of bacon spread out the slices of apples and the slices of onion; roll up the pastry so as to secure the bacon, etc. in it; place the bolster pudding in a cloth, tied at each end, and let it boil for two hours in a two-gallon pot, with plenty of water.

JULIAN WILSON
•
BAKED EGG WITH SWEETCORN

Ingredients
To serve 1–2 ✕

Metric/Imperial		American
1	small can of creamed sweetcorn	1
2	eggs	2
4	bacon slices	4
2	tomatoes	2
100 g/4 oz	mushrooms (optional)	1 cup

Method
Preheat the oven to 180°C/350°F/Gas 4.

Divide the sweetcorn between two individual baking dishes, such as small gratin dishes. Make a well in each dish of sweetcorn and into this break an egg.

Remove any rind from the bacon; halve the tomatoes. Arrange the bacon and tomatoes in the dishes around the egg. If there is room, add a few mushrooms too.

Bake until the eggs are set and the other ingredients are cooked and piping hot.

103

JAMES HERRIOT
●
PANACALTY

Ingredients
To serve 4 ✗✗

Metric/ Imperial		American
3	large potatoes	3
225 g/8 oz	bacon	½ lb
1	large onion	1
	salt and pepper	
300 ml/½ pint	water	1¼ cups

Method

Peel and thinly slice the potatoes. Remove any rind from the bacon slices. Peel and finely chop the onion.

Put a layer of potato slices over the bottom of a non-stick frying pan with a few drops of water. Add a layer of bacon slices and sprinkle with a layer of onion. Add seasoning to taste. Continue layering the ingredients until all are used up. Add the water.

Cover the pan and cook until the potatoes are tender.

JOHN HANSON
●
STUFFED MARROW [SQUASH]

Ingredients
To serve 3–4 ✗✗✗

Metric/ Imperial		American
1	large marrow [summer squash]	1
1	onion	1
450 g/1 lb	lean minced [ground] beef	1 lb
225 g/8 oz	tomatoes	½ lb
	gravy powder	
25 g/1 oz	melted butter	2 tbsp
	salt and pepper	

Method

Preheat the oven to 180°C/350°F/Gas 4.

Peel the marrow [squash] and scrape out the seeds. Set aside.

Peel and chop the onion. Cook the onion with the beef in a saucepan until the beef is brown and crumbly. Meanwhile, peel and chop the tomatoes. Add them to the pan and continue cooking until the onion is soft and the tomatoes are pulpy. If necessary thicken with a little gravy powder.

Stuff the marrow [squash] with the beef mixture. Brush the marrow [squash] with melted butter and sprinkle with seasoning to taste. Place in a baking dish. Cover and bake for about 1 hour or until tender but still firm. Serve hot, with new potatoes and green beans.

NICHOLAS PARSONS
•
BAKED LASAGNE

Ingredients
To serve 4 ✗ ✗

Metric/ Imperial		American
2	garlic cloves	2
2 tbsp	cooking oil	2 tbsp
450 g/1 lb	minced [ground] beef	1 lb
400-g/14-oz	can of tomatoes	16-oz
4 tbsp	tomato purée [paste]	1/4 cup
1/2 tsp	dried mixed herbs	1/2 tsp
1 tsp	sugar	1 tsp
	salt and pepper	
225 g/8 oz	lasagne sheets	1/2 lb
275 g/10 oz	Gouda cheese	10 oz

Method
Peel and crush the garlic. Heat the oil in a saucepan and cook the beef and garlic until the beef is browned and crumbly. Add the tomatoes, tomato purée [paste], herbs, sugar and seasoning to taste. Simmer for 20 minutes, stirring occasionally.

Preheat the oven to 190°C/375°F/Gas 5.

Cook the sheets of pasta in boiling water until just tender. Drain on kitchen paper towels. Thinly slice 225 g/8 oz of the cheese; grate the remainder.

Make alternate layers of lasagne sheets, sliced cheese and beef sauce in a buttered baking dish, ending with the sauce. Sprinkle the grated cheese over the top.

Bake for 20 minutes and serve hot.

TRACEY ULLMAN
•
POLISH SNACK

Ingredients
To serve 1 ✗

Metric/ Imperial		American
1	small onion	1
100 g/4 oz	minced [ground] beef	1/4 lb
1	egg	1
	salt	
	rye bread	
1	bunch of watercress	1

Method
Peel and finely chop the onion. Mix the onion with the raw beef and egg and add salt to taste. Serve on rye bread with plenty of watercress.

'This is very Polish, and definitely an acquired taste.'
TRACEY ULLMAN

RON GREENWOOD
•
SPAGHETTI WITH CURRIED BEEF SAUCE

Ingredients
To serve 4 ☒

Metric/ Imperial		American
2–3	carrots	2–3
2	onions	2
450 g/1 lb	best minced [ground] beef	1 lb
300 ml/1/2 pint	beef stock	1 1/4 cups
50 g/2 oz	raisins	2 oz
1 tsp	curry powder	1 tsp
dash	Worcestershire sauce	dash
1 tsp	Marmite (yeast extract)	1 tsp
	salt and pepper	
450 g/1 lb	spaghetti	1 lb

Method

Peel and chop the carrots and onions. Cook the beef in a saucepan until it is browned and crumbly. Add the carrots, onions, beef stock, a few raisins, some curry powder, a touch of Worcestershire sauce, a little Marmite, and seasoning to taste. Bring to the boil and simmer for about 30 minutes, covered.

Cook the spaghetti in boiling water until just tender. Drain and serve with the beef sauce.

'This is my favourite recipe, which I can manage well on my own. I find it a most enjoyable meal.' RON GREENWOOD

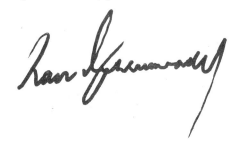

GEORGE COLE
•
STUFFED PEPPERS

Ingredients
To serve 4 ☒☒

Metric/ Imperial		American
4	sweet green peppers	4
75 g/3 oz	long-grain rice	1/2 cup
2	onions	2
100 g/4 oz	mushrooms	1 cup
350 g/12 oz	minced [ground] beef	3/4 lb
1 tsp	paprika	1 tsp
dash	Worcestershire sauce	dash
	salt and pepper	
4–8	slices of cheese	4–8

Method

Preheat the oven to 180°C/350°F/Gas 4.

Cut the tops off the peppers. Remove the seeds and white ribs. Blanch the peppers and tops in boiling water for 5 minutes. Drain and set aside.

Cook the rice in boiling water for 8 minutes. Meanwhile, peel and chop the onions. Chop the mushrooms. Cook the beef with the onions until the beef is browned and crumbly. Add the mushrooms. Drain the rice and add to the pan. Add the paprika, four slurps of Worcestershire sauce and seasoning to taste. Stir well and cook for about 10 minutes.

Fill the peppers with the beef mixture and replace the tops. Place the peppers in a baking dish and surround with the remainder of the beef mixture. Cover the lot with slices of cheese. Bake for 30–35 minutes.

'If you're courting or over 40, double the paprika!' GEORGE COLE

IAN McCASKILL
•
SPAGHETTI SAUCE

Ingredients
To serve 4 ✗ ✗

Metric/ Imperial		American
1	large onion	1
1	garlic clove	1
2 tbsp	cooking oil	2 tbsp
1	bay leaf	1
450 g/1 lb	minced [ground] steak	1 lb
700 g/1½ lb	tomatoes	1½ lb
1	sweet green pepper	1
1	celery stalk	1
1–2	carrots (optional)	1–2
1	small can of tomato purée [paste]	1
pinch	dried marjoram	pinch
pinch	dried thyme	pinch
	salt and pepper	

Method

Peel and finely chop the onion. Peel and crush the garlic. Heat the oil in a saucepan and cook the onion, garlic and bay leaf until the onion is soft. Add the beef and cook until browned and crumbly.

Meanwhile, peel and chop the tomatoes. Core, seed and chop the green pepper. Chop the celery. Peel and dice the carrots, if using.

Add all the prepared vegetables to the pan. Add the tomato purée [paste] and stir well. Add herbs and seasoning to taste. Simmer on a low heat for 45 minutes, stirring occasionally.

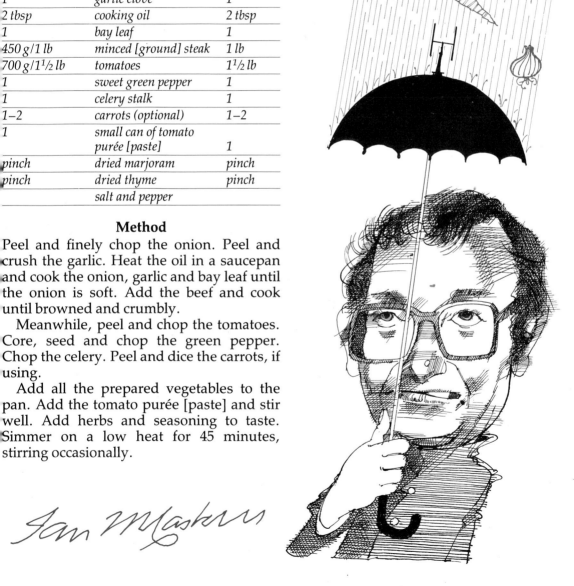

Ian McCaskill

JIMMY CARTER
•
'PLAINS SPECIAL' CHEESE RING

Ingredients
To serve 6–8 ✗✗

Metric/		
Imperial		American
450 g/1 lb	mature [sharp] cheese	1 lb
100 g/4 oz	finely chopped nuts	1 cup
250 ml/8 fl oz	mayonnaise	1 cup
1	small onion	1
1 pinch	cayenne pepper	1 pinch
	black pepper	
150 g/5–6 oz	strawberry preserves (optional)	½ cup

Method
Grate the cheese and place it in a mixing bowl. Add the nuts and mayonnaise. Peel and finely grate the onion and add to the bowl. Add a pinch of cayenne pepper, and black pepper to taste. Mix well together.

Shape the mixture into a ball, flattened disc or square, or other shape as desired. Alternatively, press into a ring mould. Cover and chill until firm.

If chilled in a ring mould, turn out and fill the centre with strawberry preserves. Serve with savoury biscuits [crackers].

OFFICE OF
JIMMY CARTER

DAVID STEEL
•
WELSH RAREBIT

Ingredients
To serve 4 ✗

Metric/		
Imperial		American
225 g/8 oz	Cheddar or Cheshire cheese	½ lb
½ tsp	dry mustard	½ tsp
½ tsp	paprika	½ tsp
½ tsp	cayenne pepper	½ tsp
	salt	
1	small can of beer or stout	1
4 slices	hot buttered toast	4 slices

Method
Shred the cheese and put it in a double boiler. Let it melt slowly over hot water kept just under boiling point. Add the mustard, paprika, cayenne and salt to taste according to the needs of the cheese. Gradually stir in as much beer or stout as the cheese will absorb. The mixture should be smooth and velvety.

Serve on hot buttered toast.

CATHERINE COOKSON
•
AMERICAN BITE

Ingredients
To serve 1 ✘

Metric/ Imperial		American
2	wheat crispbreads	2
25 g/1/2 oz	butter	1 tbsp
50 g/1 oz	large raisins	1 tbsp
1	apple	1
	pieces of assorted cheeses to taste	

Method
Butter the crispbreads. Arrange on a plate with the raisins, apple cut into wedges and cheese. Wash down with a glass of wine.

PETER BOWLES
•
CHEESE AND TOMATO TOASTY

Ingredients
To serve 1 ✘

Metric/ Imperial		American
1	slice of brown or white bread	1
25 g/1/2 oz	butter	1 tbs
2	slices of tomato	2
2	slices of blue Cheshire cheese	2
2	slices of salami	2

Method
Preheat the grill [broiler].

Toast one side of the bread, then butter the untoasted side. Place on it the tomato and cheese slices and then the salami. Put it under the grill [broiler] and cook until the cheese melts.

DEREK JACOBI
•
CHEESE AND POTATO PIE

Ingredients
To serve 4 ✘ ✘

Metric/ Imperial		American
1 kg/2 lb	potatoes	2 lb
225 g/8 oz	grated Cheddar cheese	2 cups
300 ml/1/2 pint	milk	1 1/4 cups
25–50 g/ 1–2 oz	butter	2–4 tbsp
2	eggs	2
	salt and pepper	

Method
Preheat the oven to 180°C/350°F/Gas 4.

Peel the potatoes and cut them into thin slices. Make alternate layers of potatoes and cheese in a greased baking dish, finishing with cheese.

Heat the milk with the butter until the butter has melted. Lightly beat the eggs. Add the milk mixture and season to taste with salt and pepper. Mix well.

Pour the egg and milk mixture into the baking dish. Bake for about 1 hour. Serve hot.

Variations: Add any or all of the following: 1 onion, grated or finely chopped, 1–2 tomatoes, sliced, or 75 g/3 oz bacon, chopped and fried.

109

DESSERTS

JAMES PRIOR
•
BANANA ICE CREAM

Ingredients
To serve 4 ✖✖✖

Metric/ Imperial		American
1	egg	1
2 tbsp	caster [superfine] sugar	2 tbsp
4	large ripe bananas	4
1	lemon	1
600 ml/1 pint	double [heavy] cream	2½ cups

Method

Beat the egg with the sugar until pale and the sugar has dissolved. Peel and mash the bananas and blend with the egg mixture. Add the juice of the lemon and half the cream. Pour into a freezerproof container and freeze for 1½ hours.

Beat the banana mixture well to break down the ice crystals. Whip the remaining cream and fold into the banana mixture. Freeze for a further 1½ hours or until firm.

ROBERT ROBINSON
•
BRANDY BANANAS

Ingredients
To serve 4 ✖

Metric/ Imperial		American
4–8	bananas	4–8
50 g/2 oz	butter	¼ cup
50 g/2 oz	brown sugar	⅓ cup
	brandy	

Method

Peel the bananas and cut them in half lengthways. Heat a little butter in a frying pan and fry the strips of banana gently. Sprinkle with brown sugar. When the sugar has melted and the bananas are golden in colour, pour on a spoonful or two of brandy (or whisky, rum or sherry) and serve hot or cold.

FRANKIE HOWERD
•
COLD LEMON SOUFFLÉ

Ingredients
To serve 4 ✗✗✗

Metric/ Imperial		American
4	eggs	4
225 g/8 oz	caster [superfine] sugar	1 cup
2	lemons	2
1 sachet	unflavoured powdered gelatine	1 envelope
3 tbsp	water	2 tbsp
300 ml/½ pint	whipping cream	1 cup
	To decorate	
	grated chocolate	
	slivered almonds	

Method
Separate the eggs. Place the yolks in a mixing bowl and add the sugar. Finely grate the rind from the lemons and squeeze out the juice. Add the lemon rind and juice to the bowl. Place over a pan of hot water and beat until the mixture is pale and very thick. Remove from the hot water. (If using an electric mixer, no heat is needed.)

Dissolve the gelatine in the water and add to the lemon mixture. Whip the cream and fold all but about 2 tbsp into the mixture. Beat the egg whites until stiff and fold in.

Tie a band of buttered greaseproof [wax] paper around a soufflé dish so that it rises about 7.5 cm/3 in above the rim. Spoon the lemon mixture into the dish. Chill until set.

When ready to serve, carefully peel off the paper collar. Sprinkle grated chocolate on top of the soufflé and press the almonds onto the sides. Finish with a piped rosette of the reserved cream in the centre of the top.

SHIRLEY WILLIAMS
•
LEMON PUDDING

Ingredients
To serve 4 ✗✗✗

Metric/ Imperial		American
1	large lemon	1
225 g/8 oz	self raising flour	2 cups
100 g/4 oz	shredded suet	½ cup
100 g/4 oz	brown sugar	⅔ cup

Method
Grate the rind from the lemon, taking care not to include any of the white pith. Set the rind and lemon aside.

Mix the flour and suet with enough water to make a soft dough. Roll out about two-thirds of the dough to 2-cm/¾-in thick and use to line a round pie dish that is 10-cm/4-in deep. Place the lemon in the dish. Mix the lemon rind with the brown sugar and pack around the lemon. Roll out the remaining dough and cover the dish, sealing the edges well.

Steam for 1½–2 hours, and serve hot.

FRANCES COVERDALE
•
LEMON SYLLABUB

Ingredients
To serve 6 ✗

Metric/ Imperial		American
300 ml/½ pint	double [heavy] cream	1¼ cups
100 g/4 oz	caster [superfine] sugar	½ cup
1	large lemon	1
4 tbsp	medium dry sherry	¼ cup

Method

Place the cream and sugar in a mixing bowl. Finely grate the rind from the lemon and set it aside. Squeeze the juice and strain it into the bowl. Add the sherry and beat until quite thick. Fold in the lemon rind.

Spoon into serving glasses and chill well. For colour contrast, decorate each syllabub with half a black grape and serve with sponge fingers [ladyfingers].

JULIAN LLOYD WEBBER
•
LYCHEE AND ORANGE COMPOTE

Ingredients
To serve 4 ✗✗

Metric/		
Imperial		American
2	oranges	2
225-g/8-oz	can of lychees	8-oz
2 tsp	arrowroot	2 tsp
1 tbsp	raisins	1 tbsp

Method

Finely grate the rind from one orange and reserve it. Peel both oranges, removing all the white pith. Separate into segments by cutting in between the membranes. Do this over a bowl to catch the juice.

Drain most of the syrup from the can of lychees into a small saucepan. Add the grated orange rind and any orange juice. Dissolve the arrowroot in the remaining lychee syrup and add to the pan. Bring to the boil, stirring, and simmer until thickened and clear. Remove from the heat and stir in the orange segments, lychees and raisins.

Allow to cool, then divide the mixture between four dessert dishes. Chill before serving.

ALAN BEITH
•
ORANGE PUDDING

Ingredients
To serve 4 ✗✗

Metric/		
Imperial		American
300 ml/¹/₂ pint	milk	1¹/₄ cups
100 g/4 oz	breadcrumbs made from day-old bread	2 cups
25 g/1 oz	butter	2 tbsp
100 g/4 oz	caster [superfine] sugar	¹/₂ cup
2	oranges	2
2	eggs	2

Method

Preheat the oven to 180°C/350°F/Gas 4.

Bring the milk to the boil. Place the breadcrumbs in a mixing bowl and pour on the boiling milk. Add the butter and half the sugar and stir well. Finely grate the rind from the oranges and stir into the mixture. Allow to cool.

Squeeze the juice from the oranges. Separate the eggs. Add the orange juice and egg yolks to the mixture and beat well to blend. Pour into a well-greased baking dish.

Beat the egg whites until frothy. Gradually beat in the remaining sugar and continue beating until the meringue is stiff and glossy. Spread on top of the orange mixture, to the sides of the dish, and pull the meringue up into peaks.

Bake for 30 minutes, and serve hot.

RONNIE CORBETT
•
BAKED APPLE AND ALMOND PUDDING

Ingredients
To serve 4 ✗✗

Metric/ Imperial		American
450 g/1 lb	cooking apples	1 lb
50 g/2 oz	brown sugar	⅓ cup
1–2 tbsp	water	1–2 tbsp
100 g/4 oz	butter	½ cup
100 g/4 oz	caster [superfine] sugar	½ cup
2 eggs	eggs	2
100 g/4 oz	ground almonds	1 cup

Method

Preheat the oven to 180°C/350°F/Gas 4.

Peel, core and slice the apples. Place them in a saucepan and add the brown sugar and water. Simmer gently until soft, stirring occasionally.

Meanwhile, cream the butter with the caster [superfine] sugar until light and fluffy. Beat in the eggs. Fold in the ground almonds.

Spoon the apples into a buttered 900-ml/ 1½-pint [1-quart] baking dish and smooth them out. Spread over the creamed almond mixture. Bake for 1 hour. Serve hot with cream.

'I try to eat as few sweets as I can keep my weight down, but if I do ever have a sweet, this is one I enjoy thoroughly.'
RONNIE CORBETT

HAROLD WILSON
•
APPLE CHARLOTTE

Ingredients
To serve 4 ✗✗

Metric/ Imperial		American
450 g/1 lb	cooking apples	1 lb
75 g/3 oz	butter	6 tbsp
75 g/3 oz	sugar	6 tbsp
½ loaf	stale white bread, sliced	½ loaf
½	lemon	½
3	egg yolks	3

Method

Peel, core and slice the apples. Place them in a saucepan and add 25 g/1 oz [2 tbsp] of the butter and the sugar. Cook until the apples are pulped, stirring occasionally.

Preheat the oven to 200°C/400°F/Gas 6.

Melt the remaining butter. Remove any crusts from the bread. Dip the bread into the butter to coat lightly, then use to line the bottom and sides of a baking dish or ovenproof mould. Keep the neatest pieces of bread for the top.

When the apples are cooked, sieve them to make a smooth purée. Finely grate the rind from the ½ lemon and squeeze out the juice. Add the rind and juice to the apple purée with the egg yolks and beat well to blend. Pour into the bread-lined dish and arrange the reserved pieces of bread on top.

Bake for 45 minutes, and serve hot.

PETER JONES
•
APPLE AND MINCEMEAT CRUMBLE

Ingredients
To serve 4 ✗ ✗

Metric/ Imperial		American
450 g/1 lb	cooking apples	1 lb
225 g/8 oz	mincemeat	1 cup
75 g/3 oz	flour	¾ cup
75 g/3 oz	granulated sugar	6 tbsp
75 g/3 oz	butter or margarine	6 tbsp
	brown sugar	

Method
Preheat the oven to 180°C/350°F/Gas 4.

Peel, core and slice the apples. Put them in a saucepan with a little water and cover with buttered greaseproof [wax] paper or foil and the lid. Cook until tender, stirring occasionally.

Meanwhile, spread a layer of mincemeat over the bottom of a buttered baking dish.

Rub together the flour, granulated sugar and butter or margarine until crumbly.

When the apples are cooked, sweeten with brown sugar to taste. Put them into the baking dish on top of the mincemeat and sprinkle over the crumble topping. Bake for about 30 minutes. Serve hot with cream – better still – ice cream.

'You can prepare this dish well in advance of your meal – even the day before. Then, just as you are sitting down to your first course, pop it in the oven and it will ready by the time it's needed.' PETER JONES

RICHARD BRIERS
•
CARAMEL AND APPLE SOUFFLÉ

Ingredients
To serve 4 ✗ ✗

Metric/ Imperial		American
500 g/1¼ lb	cooking apples	1¼ lb
4 tbsp	water	¼ cup
½	lemon	½
25 g/1 oz	granulated sugar	2 tbsp
50 g/2 oz	cream cheese, at room temperature	2 oz (¼ cup)
300 ml/½ pint	double [heavy] cream	1¼ cups
	demerara [light brown] sugar	

Method
Peel, core and slice the apples. Place them in a saucepan with the water, juice of the ½ lemon and the granulated sugar. Cook gently until the apples are soft and pulpy. Mash with a fork until fairly smooth, then allow to cool. Chill for 1 hour.

Beat the cream cheese until smooth, then beat in the apple mixture. Whip the cream until stiff and fold into the mixture. Divide between individual flameproof serving dishes and chill until required.

When ready to serve, preheat the grill [broiler].

Sprinkle the top of each desert with demerara [light brown] sugar and place under the grill [broiler] to melt the sugar and caramelize it. Serve immediately.

115

DAVID JESSEL
●
BEN AND ROBERT'S RANGAPANGA PIE

Ingredients
To serve 4–6 ✖ ✖ ✖

Metric/ Imperial		American
150 g/6 oz	crushed digestive biscuits [graham crackers]	1½ cups
75 g/3 oz	melted butter	6 tbsp
1½	lemons	1½
2	eggs	2
225 g/8 oz	condensed milk	8 oz
1 tsp	cream of tartar	1 tsp
75 g/3 oz	caster [superfine] sugar	6 tbsp

Method
Mix together the crushed biscuits [crackers] and melted butter. Press over the bottom and up the sides of a quiche or tart pan. Chill.

Preheat the oven to 150°C/300°F/Gas 2.

Grate the rind from one lemon. Squeeze the juice from all the lemons. Set aside.

Separate the eggs. Whisk the yolks until they are light yellow. Whisk in the condensed milk. Add the lemon rind and juice and cream of tartar and mix well. Pour into the crumb crust.

Beat the egg whites until stiff. Add half the sugar and continue beating until very stiff and glossy. Fold in the remaining sugar. Spoon the meringue over the lemon filling and swirl it decoratively, sealing it to the crumb crust.

Bake for about 1 hour. Delicious hot or cold, though a lot less gooey when cold.

NICK ROSS
●
MOCHA PUDDING

Ingredients
To serve many ✖ ✖ ✖

Metric/ Imperial		American
100 g/4 oz	unsalted butter	½ cup
100 g/4 oz	caster [superfine] sugar	½ cup
2	eggs	2
1 tbsp	coffee essence [extract]	1 tbsp
1 tbsp	coffee essence [extract]	1 tbsp
3 tbsp	dry sherry	3 tbsp
8	trifle sponge cakes [individual Mary Ann cakes]	8
150 ml/¼ pint	double [heavy] cream	½ cup
1 tbsp	chopped nuts or chocolate vermicelli [sprinkles]	1 tbsp

Method
Beat the butter and sugar together until light and creamy. Add the eggs one at a time. Beat in the coffee essence [extract] and sherry.

Cut the sponges in three, lengthwise. Arrange 2 pieces in the bottom of a basin, pour over a little of the creamed butter mixture, cover with more sponge. Continue layers until all the sponge and butter mixture are used up. Put into a cold place with a saucer and a weight on top for 3 hours.

Dip a knife into hot water and run it around the inside of the bowl. Turn the pudding out onto a dish and cover with cream. Cover with chopped nuts or chocolate vermicelli [sprinkles] just before serving.

MARIAN FOSTER
•
STRAWBERRY CARDINAL

Ingredients
To serve 6–8 ✗

Metric/ Imperial		American
900 g/2 lb	strawberries	2 lb (about 3 pints)
350 g/12 oz	raspberries	¾ lb (about 1½ pints)
50 g/2 oz	sugar	¼ cup
2 tbsp	lemon juice	2 tbsp

Method
Cut the strawberries in half or into quarters if they are very large. Use a stainless steel knife to do this as carbon steel taints the fruit. Put the strawberries in a serving bowl. Cover and chill.

Combine the raspberries, sugar and lemon juice in a stainless steel or enamel-lined saucepan and heat slowly, stirring occasionally to dissolve the sugar. Bring to the boil and simmer for 1–2 minutes – not too long or you will lose the 'fresh' flavour of the fruit. Allow to cool, then rub through a fine-meshed sieve to make a purée. Chill.

About 1 hour before serving, gently mix the strawberries with the raspberry sauce.

'This is a recipe learnt from the chef Michael Smith. It is an elegant dish, easy to make and delicious. The secret I'm told lies in cutting the strawberries in half so that they can absorb the purée.' MARIAN FOSTER

STUART BLANCH
•
FROZEN STRAWBERRY MOUSSE

Ingredients
To serve 4 ✗✗

Metric/ Imperial		American
50 g/2 oz	flour	½ cup
25 g/1 oz	brown sugar	2½ tbsp
50 g/2 oz	melted butter or margarine	¼ cup
50 g/2 oz	chopped walnuts	½ cup
1	egg white	1
100 g/4 oz	granulated sugar	½ cup
2 tsp	lemon juice	2 tsp
400-g/14-oz	can of strawberries or raspberries	16-oz
150 ml/¼ pint	double [heavy] cream	½ cup

Method
Preheat the oven to 160°C/325°F/Gas 3.

Mix together the flour, brown sugar, melted butter or margarine and walnuts. Rub together until crumbly. Spread out on a baking sheet and bake for 15 minutes. Allow to cool, then crumble the mixture by hand onto the bottom of a shallow freezer-proof dish. Set aside.

Put the egg white, granulated sugar and lemon juice into a mixing bowl. Drain the berries and add them. Beat for a good 5 minutes. Whip the cream until thick and fold into the berry mixture. Spoon into the dish on top of the crumbled mixture. Cover and freeze.

About 10 minutes before serving, remove the mousse from the freezer to allow it to soften slightly.

117

JEAN ROGERS
•
BAKED PEACHES WITH ORANGE SAUCE

Ingredients
To serve 4 ✘✘

Metric/ Imperial		American
4	ripe peaches	4
50 g/2 oz	butter	1/4 cup
50 g/2 oz	brown sugar	1/3 cup
3	oranges	3
2	lemons	2
1 tsp	cornflour [cornstarch]	1 tsp
1 tbsp	Cointreau	1 tbsp

Method
Preheat the oven to 180°C/350°F/Gas 4.

If liked, blanch the peaches in boiling water and then peel them. With a sharp knife and spoon, remove the stone [pit] from each peach, working from the stem end and keeping the peach as intact as possible. Put a small piece of butter and 1 tsp brown sugar in the hole in each peach. Arrange them in a small baking dish and bake for 30 minutes.

Meanwhile, finely grate the rind from one orange and one lemon. Squeeze the juice from all the oranges and lemons. Combine the grated rinds and juices in a saucepan and add 2 tbsp brown sugar. Bring to the boil, stirring to dissolve the sugar. Dissolve the cornflour [cornstarch] in the Cointreau and add to the pan. Simmer, stirring, until smooth and thickened.

Pour the sauce over the peaches and serve, with cream if liked.

VALERIE SINGLETON
•
TOFFEE-TOPPED PEACHES AND CREAM

Ingredients
To serve 4 ✘

Metric/ Imperial		American
4	ripe peaches	4
	kirsch or Cointreau	
150 ml/1/4 pint	double [heavy] cream	3/4 cup
100g/4 oz	demerara [light brown] sugar	2/3 cup

Method
Peel the peaches and remove the stones [pits]. Cut the peaches into slices and place in a flameproof serving dish. Sprinkle with the kirsch or Cointreau. Cover and chill overnight.

The next day, preheat the grill [broiler].

Whip the cream and spread over the peaches. Sprinkle the sugar in a thick layer over the cream. Put the dish under the grill [broiler] and cook until the sugar melts and caramelizes. Allow to cool before serving.

JEREMY MOORE
•
GOOSEBERRY TART

Ingredients

To serve 4–6 ✗✗

Metric/ Imperial		American
225 g/8 oz	flour	2 cups
100 g/4 oz	caster [superfine] sugar	1/2 cup
100 g/4 oz	butter	1/2 cup
1	egg	1
1 1/2 tsp	milk	1 1/2 tsp
1 1/2 tsp	vinegar	1 1/2 tsp
450 g/1 lb	fresh gooseberries	1 lb
2	egg yolks	2
150 ml/1/4 pint	single [light] cream	1/2 cup

Method

Sift the flour into a bowl. Add 2 tbsp of the sugar and the butter and rub together until the mixture resembles crumbs. Add the whole egg, the milk and vinegar and bind to a soft dough. If necessary, add more milk or a little water to help bind. Wrap and chill for 1 hour.

Preheat the oven to 220°C/425°F/Gas 7.

Roll out the dough and use to line a 20-cm/8-in quiche or tart pan. Prick the bottom and bake blind for 10 minutes.

Meanwhile, top and tail the gooseberries. Lightly beat together the egg yolks, cream and remaining sugar.

Pack the gooseberries into the pastry case and pour over the cream mixture. Reduce the oven temperature to 190°C/375°F/Gas 5 and bake the tart for 30–40 minutes or until the filling is set. Serve hot or cold.

TORVILL and DEAN
•
WEINACHT'S CREAM

Ingredients
To serve 4–6 ✖✖

Metric/ Imperial		American
100 g/4 oz	stoned [pitted] prunes	⅓ cup
	rum	
75 g/3 oz	walnuts	¾ cup
100 g/4 oz	granulated sugar	½ cup
300 ml/½ pint	milk	1¼
2	eggs	2
2	egg yolks	2
150 g/5 oz	caster [superfine] sugar	⅔ cup
	vanilla essence [extract]	
300 ml/½ pint	whipping cream	1¼ cups

Method

Finely chop the prunes and place them in a bowl. Cover with rum. Leave overnight.

Chop the walnuts coarsely. Place them in a saucepan with the granulated sugar and cook over a moderate heat, stirring occasionally, until the sugar has melted. Continue cooking until the sugar has caramelized and coated the walnuts. Pour the mixture onto an oiled baking sheet and leave to cool and set. When cold, crush this praline.

Drain the prunes, discarding the rum.

Put the milk, eggs, egg yolks, caster [superfine] sugar and 2 drops of vanilla in a heatproof bowl. Place the bowl over a pan of hot water and beat until the mixture is very thick; when dripped back onto the surface of the mixture from the beaters, the drop should stay on the surface for 2 seconds.

Remove the bowl from over the hot water and continue beating until cold.

Whip the cream until thick but not stiff and fold into the mixture with the prunes. Before serving, sprinkle over the praline.

KENNETH WILLIAMS
•
PRUNE MOULD

Ingredients
To serve 4 ✖✖✖

Metric/ Imperial		American
450 g/1 lb	prunes	1 lb
	cloves	
	piece of lemon rind	
1 sachet	unflavoured powdered gelatine	1 envelope
100 g/4 oz	caster [superfine] sugar	½ cup

Method

Soak the prunes in water to cover overnight.

The next day, tip the prunes and their soaking water into a saucepan and add a few cloves and the piece of lemon rind. Cook gently until the prunes are very soft.

Drain the prunes, reserving the liquid. Discard the cloves and lemon rind. Stone [pit] the prunes and, if liked, sieve them to a purée. Alternatively, blend until smooth in a blender or food processor.

If there is not 300 ml/½ pint [1¼ cups] of reserved cooking liquid, add a little water. Dissolve the gelatine and sugar in the liquid. Stir in the prunes. Pour into individual moulds and chill until set.

Turn out to serve, with cream or custard sauce.

'Fun moulds can be used for this – animal shapes, etc.'
KENNETH WILLIAMS

MEL SMITH
•
BLACKCURRANT SORBET

Ingredients
To serve 6 ✗✗✗

Metric/ Imperial		American
350 g/12 oz	fresh or frozen blackcurrants	¾ lb (about 1½ pints)
350 ml/12 fl oz	water	1½ cups
100 g/4 oz	caster [superfine] sugar	½ cup
2 tsp	lemon juice	2 tsp
2	egg whites	2

Method

Top and tail the blackcurrants. Put the blackcurrants in a saucepan with 3 tbsp of the water. Cook gently until the fruit becomes pulpy. Allow to cool slightly, then rub through a nylon sieve using a wooden spoon. Set aside.

Put the sugar and remaining water in a heavy saucepan and bring to the boil, stirring to dissolve the sugar. Boil the syrup until it reaches the thread stage (115°C/230–234°F on a sugar thermometer). Allow the syrup to cool completely.

Stir the syrup into the blackcurrant purée with the lemon juice. Pour the mixture into a freezerproof container and freeze for about 1½ hours or until mushy.

Beat the mixture thoroughly to break down ice crystals. Beat the egg whites until stiff and fold into the blackcurrant mixture. Freeze again, beating once more after 1 hour, until firm.

KATIE BOYLE
•
CHOCOLATE POTS

Ingredients
To serve 4–6 ✗

Metric/ Imperial		American
175 g/6 oz	plain [semisweet] chocolate	6 squares
2 tbsp	cream	2 tbsp
3	eggs	3

Method

Place the chocolate and cream in the top of a double boiler or in a bowl placed over a pan of simmering water. Heat until melted and smooth, stirring occasionally. Remove from the heat.

Separate the eggs. Beat the yolks into the chocolate mixture. Beat the egg whites until stiff and fold into the mixture. Spoon into little dishes and chill. Serve topped with whipped cream, if liked.

'The added advantage of this recipe is that it keeps for days.'
KATIE BOYLE

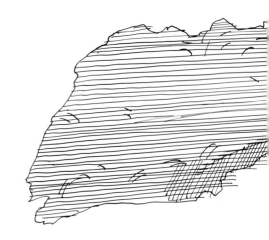

DENIS HEALEY
•
RHUBARB FOOL

Ingredients
To serve 4 ✖✖

Metric/		
Imperial		*American*
450 g/1 lb	*rhubarb*	*1 lb*
100 g/4 oz	*sugar*	*¹/₂ cup*
100 ml/¹/₂ pint	*whipping cream*	*1¹/₄ cups*

Method

Trim the rhubarb and cut it into small pieces. Place in a saucepan with the sugar and cook gently until very soft, stirring occasionally. Remove from the heat and allow to cool. If liked, sieve the rhubarb to make a purée, or blend in a blender or food processor. Taste and add more sugar if necessary.

Whip the cream and fold into the rhubarb. Spoon into dessert glasses, and chill well before serving.

ANNE KIRKBRIDE

•

LAYERED CHOCOLATE SOUFFLÉ

Ingredients
To serve 6 ✗✗

Metric/ Imperial		American
3	eggs	3
100 g/4 oz	caster [superfine] sugar	½ cup
6 tbsp	water	6 tbsp
1 sachet	unflavoured powdered gelatine	1 envelope
125 g/5 oz	plain [semisweet] chocolate	5 squares
225-g/8-oz	can of evaporated milk	8-oz

Method

Separate the eggs. Place the yolks in a mixing bowl and add the sugar and half the water. Beat until the mixture is thick and creamy and will form a ribbon trail on itself when the beaters are lifted out. (If not using an electric mixer, beat the mixture in a bowl placed over a pan of hot water.) Dissolve the gelatine in the remaining water.

Melt 50 g/2 oz [2 squares] of the chocolate, and grate the remaining chocolate.

Add the melted chocolate and gelatine to the egg yolk mixture and blend together well.

Whisk the evaporated milk until thick and fold into the mixture. Beat the egg whites until stiff and fold in.

Pour some of the mixture into a large glass serving bowl and sprinkle with a layer of grated chocolate. Cover with another layer of the soufflé mixture and sprinkle again with grated chocolate. Continue layering, and finish with grated chocolate. Chill before serving, topped with whipped cream.

SUE LAWLEY

•

ARGENTAN

Ingredients
To serve 6–8 ✗✗

Metric/ Imperial		American
225 g/8 oz	unsalted butter	1 cup
125 g/5 oz	caster [superfine] sugar	⅔ cup
225 g/8 oz	plain [semisweet] chocolate	8 squares
2 tbsp	brandy or Cointreau	2 tbsp
5	eggs	5
225 g/8 oz	crushed semisweet biscuits [cookies]	2 cups

Method

Cream the butter with the sugar until light and fluffy. Melt the chocolate with the brandy or Cointreau in a heavy saucepan over a very gentle heat. When smooth, beat into the creamed mixture. Separate the eggs and beat the yolks into the mixture. Stir in the crushed biscuits [cookies].

Beat the egg whites until stiff and fold into the mixture. Spoon into a foil-lined cake pan. Smooth the top. Cover and chill overnight.

ROY CASTLE
•
CHOCOLATE PARTY GÂTEAU

Ingredients

To serve 6–8 ✗✗

Metric/ Imperial		American
6	trifle sponge cakes [individual Mary Ann cakes] or slices of Madeira [pound] cake	6
225 g/8 oz	plain [semisweet] chocolate	8 squares
3 tbsp	top-of-the-milk [half-and-half]	3 tbsp
3	eggs	3
2 tbsp	brandy	2 tbsp
300 ml/¹/₂ pint	double [heavy] cream	1¹/₄ cups

Method

Cut the cakes into thin slices. Set aside.

Melt 150 g/6 oz [6 squares] of the chocolate in the top of a double boiler or in a bowl placed over a pan of boiling water. Remove from the heat and stir in the top-of-the-milk [half-and-half]. Separate the eggs and beat the yolks into the chocolate mixture with the brandy. Beat the egg whites until stiff and fold into the mixture.

Line the bottom of a bowl with some of the cake slices. Add a layer of the chocolate mixture. Continue making layers until all the ingredients are used up, ending with a layer of cake slices. Cover and chill for at least 12 hours.

To serve, turn out onto a serving plate. Whip the cream and spread over the cake. Grate the remaining chocolate and sprinkle over.

CLARISSA MASON
·
GÂTEAU GAFFE

Ingredients
To serve 6–8 ✗✗

Metric/ Imperial		American
1	lemon	1
6	egg whites	6
6 tbsp	caster [superfine] sugar	6 tbsp
50 g/2 oz	sultanas [golden raisins]	⅓ cup
50 g/2 oz	raisins	⅓ cup
225 g/8 oz	desiccated [shredded] coconut	2⅔ cups
	23–25 cm/9–10 inch pastry shell	

Method
Preheat the oven to 180°C/350°F/Gas 4.

Finely grate the rind from the lemon and squeeze out the juice. Combine the lemon rind and juice, egg whites and sugar in a mixing bowl and beat until very thick and glossy – about 10 minutes. Add the sultanas [golden raisins], raisins and coconut and fold in gently but thoroughly.

Pour the mixture into the pastry shell. Bake for about 30 minutes or until brown.

'The result is not precisely what I had intended – hence the name.' CLARISSA MASON

DIANE HOLLAND
·
PASCHA

Ingredients
To serve 6–8 ✗✗✗

Metric/ Imperial		American
900 g/2 lb	curd [cottage] cheese	2 lb (4 cups)
225 g/8 oz	sugar	1 cup
5 tbsp	single [light] cream	5 tbsp
150 ml/¼ pint	plain yogurt	½ cup
	vanilla essence [extract]	
100 g/4 oz	sultanas [golden raisins]	⅔ cup
75 g/3 oz	currants	½ cup
75 g/3 oz	chopped candied peel	½ cup

Method
If necessary, sieve the cheese to make it smooth. Add the sugar and beat until it has dissolved. Gradually mix in the cream and yogurt. Add 4 or 5 drops of vanilla essence [extract]. Fold in the raisins, currants and peel.

Line a cheese mould, colander, sieve or waxed carton punctured all over the bottom and sides with muslin or cheesecloth. Spoon in the cheese mixture and fold the muslin or cheesecloth over. Place a weight on top. Leave in a cool place to drain for at least 24 hours.

To serve, turn out onto a serving plate and remove the muslin or cheesecloth.

GLENDA JACKSON
•
CASSATA DI MASCAPONI

Ingredients
To serve 6 ✖✖✖

Metric/ Imperial		American
225 g/8 oz	cream cheese, at room temperature	½ lb
150 ml/¼ pint	cream	½ cup
2	eggs	2
50 g/2 oz	caster [superfine] sugar	¼ cup
2 tbsp	rum	2 tbsp

Method

Beat the cream cheese with the cream until smooth. Separate the eggs and beat the yolks with the sugar until the sugar has dissolved. Add the rum. Add the egg yolk mixture to the cream cheese mixture and blend until smooth. Beat the egg whites until stiff and fold into the mixture.

Spoon into a freezerproof mould. Freeze for 2–3 hours. Eat the day of making.

'This is a delicious pudding!' GLENDA JACKSON

ANGELA THORNE
•
CRÈME BRÛLÉE

Ingredients
To serve 4 ✖✖✖

Metric/ Imperial		American
4	egg yolks	4
50 g/2 oz	caster [superfine] sugar	¼ cup
300 ml/½ pint	double [heavy] cream	1¼ cups
300 ml/½ pint	single [light] cream	1¼ cups
	vanilla essence [extract]	
75 g/3 oz	granulated sugar	6 tbsp
3 tbsp	water	3 tbsp

Method

Preheat the oven to 150°C/300°F/Gas 2.

Combine the egg yolks and caster [superfine] sugar in a bowl and beat together lightly until the sugar has dissolved. Add the cream and a few drops of vanilla essence [extract] and blend well. Strain the custard into a 900-ml/1½-pint [1-quart] baking dish.

Place the dish in a roasting pan containing 2.5 cm/1 in hot water. Bake for 45 minutes or until the custard is just firm. Allow to cool, then chill overnight.

The next day, put the granulated sugar and water in a heavy saucepan and bring to the boil, stirring to dissolve the sugar. Boil until the syrup turns a pale caramel colour. Quickly pour three-quarters of the caramel over the top of the cold custard in an even layer. Pour the remainder of the caramel onto a well-oiled baking sheet. Allow to cool and set.

Crush the sheet of caramel and arrange around the top of the caramel-coated custard before serving.

PAUL HEINEY
•
PLUM DUFF

Ingredients
To serve 4–6 ✗✗✗

Metric/ Imperial		American
100 g/4 oz	flour	1 cup
100 g/4 oz	fresh breadcrumbs	2 cups
175 g/6 oz	mixed nuts	1½ cups
1 tsp	baking powder	1 tsp
50–75 g/ 2–3 oz	sugar	4–6 tbsp
	handful of raisins	
1	egg	1
150 ml/¼ pint	milk	½ cup

Method
Put the flour and breadcrumbs into a bowl. Finely chop the nuts and add with the baking powder, sugar, raisins and egg. Add enough milk to bind the ingredients. (You may need more milk.)

Place in a pudding basin [steaming mold] and cover, or wrap in a pudding cloth and tie at the top. Steam or boil for at least 2 hours. Serve hot.

'Writing as a yachtsman, I must state my position. Food tastes best when it has been earned and no food can taste finer than at the end of a long, tough passage through a damp and chill night. To ward off the effects of wind and weather, I cannot recommend too highly this recipe for Plum Duff. The exact amount of the ingredients or the omission of some of them is not necessarily of vital importance.' PAUL HEINEY

MIRIAM STOPPARD
•
SUMMER PUDDING

Ingredients
To serve 6 ✗✗

Metric/ Imperial		American
450 g/1 lb	raspberries	1 lb (about 2 pints)
450 g/1 lb	strawberries	1 lb (about 1½ pints)
225 g/8 oz	redcurrants	½ lb (about 1 pint)
225–450 g/ 8 oz–1 lb	sugar	1–2 cups
10–15	slices of fresh wholemeal [whole wheat] bread	10–15

Method
Put the fruit in a saucepan and add sugar according to the sweetness of the fruit. (The mixture should end up sweet but tart.) Bring slowly to the boil and simmer for 2 minutes only (the fruit should be still intact but very juicy). Remove from the heat.

Remove crusts from the bread and cut the slices into triangles. Completely line a deep dish with the bread so that no spaces are left. Pour in the fruit mixture. Cover with the rest of the bread. Put a weight on top and chill for 24 hours.

Turn out onto a serving dish and serve with cream.

'This can be stored in the freezer for several months – we're still eating the puddings I made last summer. One of the delights of this pudding is that the bread soaks up the juice and is a lovely rich red colour.' MIRIAM STOPPARD

SYD LAWRENCE
•
QUEEN OF PUDDINGS

Ingredients
To serve 4 ✗✗

Metric/ Imperial		American
600 ml/1 pint	milk	2½ cups
½	lemon	½
	salt	
50 g/2 oz	butter	¼ cup
100 g/4 oz	fresh breadcrumbs	2 cups
50 g/2 oz	caster [superfine] sugar	¼ cup
2	eggs	2
4 tbsp	strawberry jam	¼ cup

Method
Preheat the oven to 180°C/350°F/Gas 4.

Put the milk into a saucepan. Thinly pare the rind from the ½ lemon and add to the milk. Add a pinch of salt and the butter. Heat until the butter has melted, then bring to the boil.

Place the breadcrumbs and 40 g/1½ oz [3 tbsp] of the sugar in a mixing bowl. Discard the lemon rind from the milk mixture, then pour it over the crumbs. Stir well to mix, then cover and leave to soak for 10 minutes.

Separate the eggs. Lightly beat the egg yolks into the crumb mixture. Pour into a baking dish and bake for 10 minutes.

Spread the jam over the baked pudding base. Beat the egg whites until stiff. Add the remaining sugar and continue beating for 1 minute or until very stiff and glossy. Pile this meringue on top of the jam. Return to the oven and bake for a further 5 minutes or until the meringue is lightly browned. Serve hot.

WENDY RICHARDS
•
BREAD AND BUTTER PUDDING

Ingredients
To serve 4 ✗✗

Metric/ Imperial		American
4–6	thin slices of bread	4–6
6	thick slices of bread	6
	butter	
600 ml/1 pint	milk	2½ cups
3–4 tbsp	cream	3–4 tbsp
2 tbsp	marmalade	2 tbsp
3 tbsp	sugar	3 tbsp
2	eggs	2
	brandy or orange liqueur	
2 tbsp	mixed dried fruit (raisins, etc.)	2 tbsp

Method
Preheat the oven to 200°C/400°F/Gas 6.

Line a pudding basin or ovenproof mould with the thin slices of bread, removing crusts as necessary. Cut the thick slices of bread into cubes, removing crusts, and pile into the bread-lined basin. The basin should be full of bread, loosely packed, so add more if necessary. Dot all over with nuts of butter.

Combine the milk, cream, marmalade, sugar, eggs and a good slurp of brandy or orange liqueur in a blender or food processor and blend until smooth. Stir in the dried fruit. Pour over the bread cubes in the basin. The bread should be just covered with liquid.

Bake until golden brown and well risen up like a soufflé. Serve hot with more cream or custard sauce.

BREAKFAST
AND
TEATIME

BREAKFAST IDEAS

UNA STUBBS
•
MUESLI

Ingredients
To serve 2–4 ✗ ✗ ✗

Metric/ Imperial		American
1	*mug of milk*	1
2	*mugs of rolled oats*	2
75 g/3 oz	*sultanas [golden raisins]*	½ cup
1–2 tbsp	*honey*	1–2 tbsp
1	*banana*	1
1	*apple*	1

Method
Bring the milk to the boil and pour it over the oats. Add the sultanas [golden raisins] and honey and stir well. Cover and leave to soak overnight.

The next morning, peel and chop the banana. Core and grate the apple. Add to the muesli and stir to mix. Add any choice of extras – a little plain yogurt, cream, nuts, dried apricots, etc. – although they aren't necessary.

ALAN PLATER
•
BOILED EGGS

Ingredients
To serve 1 ✗ ✗ ✗

Metric/ Imperial		American
2	*eggs (see below)*	2
	bread and butter fingers	

Method
First buy your day-old chicks. Build a small shed and a wired-in enclosure in your garden. Better still, get your husband/wife/children/good-natured friends/parents/in-laws to do these things for you. Feed the chicks on all the stuff left on the edge of plates and let them also eat any of Nature's residuals that fall into the enclosure.

Eventually you will have hens and the hens will lay some eggs. Collect these daily or better still, persuade some of the above-listed people to do it for you. When you are hungry, select two prime specimens and boil them in a pan of water. My own preference is for medium rare, which means about 3½ minutes or the time it takes the Duke Ellington Band to play 'Things Ain't What They Used To Be', plus the time it takes to remove the record from the turntable. (Double Album UAD 60001.)

You will find that eggs prepared in this way taste 500 times better than shop eggs. The secret is in the preparation.

Garnish with bread and butter fingers. If you want to know the secret of the bread, you must get in touch with Alex Glasgow.

131

ROLF HARRIS
•
BACHELOR SCRAMBLED EGGS AND TOMATOES

Ingredients
To serve 1 ✖

Metric/ Imperial		American
1	spring onion [scallion]	1
	butter or margarine	
	milk	
2	eggs	2
	salt and pepper	
1	tomato	1

Method
Preheat the grill [broiler].

Finely chop the spring onion [scallion]. Melt a small splodge of butter or margarine in a frying pan and cook the onion over a low heat for a short while, then add a slosh of milk. Don't add too much or the eggs will be watery later. Take the pan off the heat and break in the eggs. Add a dusting of salt to each egg and as much pepper as you enjoy.

Put back on a low heat while you graunch up the eggs with a wooden spoon and generously scramble them around.

Meanwhile, cut the tomato in half and place it under the grill [broiler]. Put it flat side down first and cook until the skin shrivels up and starts to go black, then turn and add a pinch of salt. Cook the flat side.

Your scrambled egg should be just starting to solidify, so take it off the heat for a tick while you pop in your two beautifully cooked tomatoes. The skin on the smooth side just comes away but you will need to cut out the core on the other half of the tomato and take off the skin. Place back on the heat while you squelch up the tomato with the wooden spoon to mix it thoroughly with the egg. Don't dry it up too much.

JOHN WELLS
•
NOURISHING MILLION CALORIE BREAKFAST

Ingredients
To serve 1 ✖

Metric/ Imperial		American
1	thickish slice of white bread	1
	fat for frying	
	marmalade	

Method
Hold one side of the bread for a few seconds under cold running water, then fry on both sides, spreading the soggy side generously with marmalade.

'Yum yum.' JOHN WELLS

TEATIME TREATS

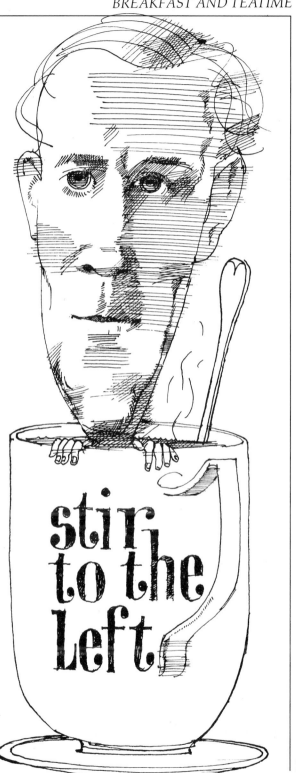

TONY BENN
•
THE PERFECT CUP OF TEA

Ingredients
To serve 1 ☒

Metric/ Imperial		American
600 ml/1 pint	spring water	2½ cups
1	Commonwealth tea bag	1
1	lump of Jamaican sugar	1

Method

Bring the water to the boil – heated by North Sea gas. Meanwhile, warm a 600-ml/ 1-pint [2½-cup] china mug.

Place the tea bag in the mug and pour in the water. Allow to steep until the strength required, then remove the tea bag. Add the sugar and stir until dissolved. To be taken hourly – or as required.

STUART HALL

●

HAZELNUT ROLLS

Ingredients

To serve 24 ⧗⧗

Metric/ Imperial		American
175 g/6 oz	onions	6 oz
4 tbsp	cooking oil	1/4 cup
175 g/6 oz	ground hazelnuts	1 1/2 cups
75 g/3 oz	porridge oats [oatmeal]	1/2 cup
2–3 tsp	Marmite (yeast extract)	2–3 tsp
1 1/2 tsp	dried mixed herbs	1 1/2 tsp
7 tbsp	water or soya milk	7 tbsp
	Pastry	
450 g/1 lb	flour	4 cups
	salt	
150 g/6 oz	butter, margarine or shortening	3/4 cup

Method

First make the pastry. Put the flour into a mixing bowl and add a large pinch of salt. Rub in the fat until the mixture resembles breadcrumbs, then add just enough cold water to bind to a dough. Wrap and chill while making the filling.

Preheat the oven to 200°C/400°F/Gas 6.

Peel and thinly slice the onions. Heat the oil in a frying pan and cook the onions until softened. Tip the onions into a mixing bowl and add the remaining filling ingredients. Mix together well. Set aside to soak for 5 minutes.

Roll out the pastry dough and cut into 10 × 15 cm/4 × 6 in rectangles. Shape the filling into rolls and place on the dough rectangles. Roll the dough around the filling and press to seal. Arrange on a baking sheet and bake for 25 minutes.

GORDON JACKSON

●

CRUMPETS

Ingredients

Makes 12 ⧗⧗

Metric/ Imperial		American
250 g/9 oz	flour	2 1/4 cups
1 tsp	salt	1 tsp
15 g/1/2 oz	fresh [compressed] yeast	1/2 oz
150 ml/1/4 pint	lukewarm milk	3/4 cup
150 ml/1/4 pint	lukewarm water	3/4 cup
1/4 tsp	bicarbonate of soda [baking soda]	1/4 tsp
4 tbsp	cold water	1/4 cup
1	egg white	1

Method

Sift the flour and salt into a mixing bowl. Crumble in the yeast. Add the lukewarm milk and water and beat vigorously for about 5 minutes to make a smooth batter. Cover and leave to rise in a warm place for about 30 minutes or until well risen.

Dissolve the soda in the cold water and beat into the batter. Beat the egg white until stiff and fold into the batter.

Grease a griddle and heat it. Grease 7.5-cm/3-in metal crumpet rings and place them on the griddle. Spoon the batter into the rings and cook until bubbles form on the surface and burst, giving an uneven pitted top. Cook on one side only. Remove from the griddle.

To serve, toast and butter.

JOHN JUNOR
•
OATCAKES

Ingredients
✗✗

Metric/ Imperial		American
225 g/8 oz	fine oatmeal	1⅓ cups
pinch	salt	pinch
pinch	bicarbonate of soda [baking soda]	pinch
25 g/1 oz	butter	2 tbsp
150 ml/¼ pint	boiling water	½ cup

Method
Preheat the oven to 180°C/350°F/Gas 4.

Place the oatmeal in a bowl and add a pinch each of salt and soda. Rub in the butter. Gradually stir in the boiling water, adding just enough to make a fairly stiff dough.

Roll out the dough to about 3-mm/⅛-in thick and place on a well-greased baking sheet. Bake for about 30 minutes.

Remove from the oven. Mark the oatcake into triangles and allow to cool. When cold, break up along the marked lines.

BARBARA WOODHOUSE
•
LEMON CAKE

Ingredients
To serve 6–8 **✗✗**

Metric/ Imperial		American
175 g/6 oz	soft margarine	¾ cup
225 g/8 oz	caster [superfine] sugar	1 cup
175 g/6 oz	self-raising flour	1¾ cups
1	large lemon	1

Method
Preheat the oven to 190°C/375°F/Gas 5.

Put the margarine, 175 g/6 oz [¾ cup] of the sugar and the flour in a mixing bowl. Finely grate the rind from the lemon and add it. Beat well with an electric mixer for about 3 minutes. Pour into a buttered 20-cm/8-in cake pan. Bake for 45 miutes.

Squeeze the juice from the lemon into a saucepan. Add the remaining sugar. Heat, stirring to dissolve the sugar. Spoon this over the cake to glaze it. Allow to cool.

GEOFFREY WHEELER
•
MINCEMEAT CAKE

Ingredients
To serve 6–8 **✗✗✗**

Metric/ Imperial		American
150 g/5 oz	butter	10 tbsp
150 g/5 oz	caster [superfine] sugar	10 tbsp
2	eggs	2
225 g/8 oz	self-raising flour	2 cups
1	jar of mincemeat	1
75 g/3 oz	currants	½ cup
	brandy	
	lemon juice	
	flaked almonds	

Method
Preheat the oven to 170°C/325°F/Gas 3.

Cream the butter and sugar until light and fluffy. Beat in the eggs. Mix in the flour, mincemeat and currants. Add a dash of brandy and a squeeze of lemon juice.

Put the mixture into a greased 20 cm/8 inch round cake pan. Sprinkle the almonds over the top. Bake for 1¾ hours or until the cake is golden brown and just beginning to shrink away from the sides of the pan. Allow to cool in the pan.

DIANE SOLOMON
•
GINGERBREAD

Ingredients
✕✕

Metric/ Imperial		American
100 g/4 oz	sugar	½ cup
1	egg	1
100 g/4 oz	butter	½ cup
275 g/10 oz	flour	2½ cups
1½ tsp	bicarbonate of soda [baking soda]	1½ tsp
1 tsp	ground cinnamon	1 tsp
1 tsp	ground ginger	1 tsp
½ tsp	salt	½ tsp
1 tbsp	grated orange rind (optional)	1 tbsp
150 g/6 oz	light molasses	½ cup
150 g/6 oz	honey	½ cup
250 ml/8 fl oz	hot water	1 cup

Method

Preheat the oven to 180°C/350°F/Gas 4.

Beat together the sugar and egg until pale and the sugar has dissolved. Melt the butter and allow it to cool, then stir into the egg mixture.

Sift the flour, soda, cinnamon, ginger and salt into another bowl. Stir in the orange rind. Mix together the molasses, honey and hot water in another bowl. Add the sifted dry ingredients and molasses mixture alternately to the egg mixture, stirring after each addition until well blended.

Pour into a greased 23-cm/9-in square baking pan. Bake for about 1 hour.

Serve warm, with whipped cream or ice cream.

JACK CHARLTON
•
BANANA CAKE

Ingredients
✕✕

Metric/ Imperial		American
225 g/8 oz	self-raising flour	2 cups
100 g/4 oz	butter or margarine	½ cup
450 g/1 lb	ripe bananas	1 lb
100 g/4 oz	brown sugar	⅔ cup
25 g/1 oz	ground almonds	¼ cup
1	egg	1
3 tbsp	milk	⅓ cup
100 g/4 oz	sultanas [golden raisins] or currants	⅔ cup
50 g/2 oz	glacé cherries	⅓ cup

Method

Preheat the oven to 160°C/325°F/Gas 3.

Sift the flour into a mixing bowl and rub in the butter or margarine until the mixture resembles crumbs. Peel and mash the bananas. Add to the bowl with the sugar and almonds and mix well. Add the egg and milk and beat until smooth, then stir in the dried fruit and cherries.

Pour into a lined loaf pan. Bake for 1 hour, then increase the oven temperature to 180°C/350°F/Gas 4 and bake for a further 30 minutes.

ROBIN COUSINS
• CARROT CAKE

Ingredients
To serve 8 ✖ ✖

Metric/ Imperial		American
6	eggs	6
225 g/8 oz	caster [superfine] sugar	1 cup
350 g/12 oz	cooked puréed carrots	1½ cups
350 g/12 oz	ground almonds	3 cups
1 tbsp	grated orange rind	1 tbsp
1 tbsp	brandy	1 tbsp

Method

Preheat the oven to 160°C/325°F/Gas 3.

Separate the eggs. Beat the egg yolks until they begin to thicken, then gradually add the sugar and beat until the mixture is thick and creamy. Add the carrot purée, ground almonds, orange rind and brandy and stir to mix thoroughly.

Beat the egg whites until stiff and fold into the carrot mixture. Pour into a buttered 23-cm/9-in loose-bottomed cake pan.

Bake for 50 minutes.

'My favourite cake is Carrot Cake which originates in America.' ROBIN COUSINS

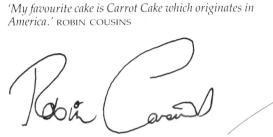

137

JIMMY KRANKIE
•
CLOOTIE DUMPLING

Ingredients
✗✗✗

Metric/ Imperial		American
250 g/9 oz	flour	2¼ cups
100 g/4 oz	shredded suet	½ cup
2 tsp	bicarbonate of soda [baking soda]	2 tsp
½ tsp	salt	½ tsp
4 tsp	ground cinnamon	4 tsp
2 tsp	ground ginger	2 tsp
½ tsp	grated nutmeg	½ tsp
1	orange	1
150 g/5 oz	sugar	⅔ cup
225 g/8 oz	currants	1⅓ cups
100 g/4 oz	sultanas [golden raisins]	⅔ cup
	milk	

Method

Sift the flour into a mixing bowl. Add the suet, soda, salt and spices and stir to mix. Finely grate the rind from the orange and add to the bowl. Add the sugar and dried fruit. Stir in enough milk to bind the ingredients.

Dampen the centre of a tea towel [dish cloth] with boiling water and dust it with flour. Put the mixture in the centre and tie up the towel around it, leaving room for the dumpling to swell.

Boil for 4–5 hours.

Drain and allow to cool before serving, cut into slices.

Jimmy Krankie

ALLISON BETTLES
•
BRANDY SNAPS

Ingredients
Makes 16 ✗✗

Metric/ Imperial		American
50 g/2 oz	butter or margarine	¼ cup
50 g/2 oz	golden syrup [light corn syrup]	3 tbsp
50 g/2 oz	sugar	¼ cup
50 g/2 oz	flour	½ cup
¼ tsp	ground ginger	¼ tsp
	salt	
½ tsp	lemon juice	½ tsp

Method

Preheat the oven to 160°C/325°F/Gas 3.

Warm the butter or margarine, syrup and sugar in a saucepan until melted and smooth. Remove from the heat. Sift the flour, ginger and a pinch of salt into a mixing bowl. Add the melted mixture and lemon juice and blend well.

Pour small spoonfuls of the mixture onto greased baking sheets, keeping the rounds well spaced as they will spread. Bake for 8 minutes.

Working quickly, lift each biscuit [cookie] – one at a time – from the baking sheet and wrap it around the greased handle of a wooden spoon. Slip the brandy snaps off the spoon as soon as they are set and cool on a wire rack. If the mixture stiffens before all the biscuits [cookies] are baked and shaped, add a few more drops of lemon juice.

If liked, fill the brandy snaps with whipped cream before serving.

DAME EDNA EVERAGE
•
AUSSIE LAMINGTONS

Ingredients
✕✕

Metric/ Imperial		American
225 g/8 oz	butter	1 cup
350 g/12 oz	sugar	1½ cups
4	eggs	4
300 ml/½ pint	milk	1¼ cups
350 g/12 oz	flour	3 cups
1 tsp	bicarbonate of soda [baking soda]	1 tsp
2 tsp	cream of tartar	2 tsp
	vanilla essence [extract]	
	glacé icing	
	desiccated [shredded] coconut	

Method

Preheat the oven to 180°C/350°F/Gas 4.

Cream the butter with the sugar until light and fluffy. Beat in the eggs, then add the milk. Sift the flour, soda and cream of tartar into the bowl. Add a few drops of vanilla essence [extract]. Blend well together.

Pour the mixture into a baking pan, about 30 × 20 cm/12 × 8 in, and bake for 30 minutes. Allow to cool. Cut the cake into squares. Coat with glacé icing, then roll in coconut.

This is my favourite recipe for Aussie lamingtons. A joyous heart always!' DAME EDNA EVERAGE

CLIFF RICHARD
•
CHRISTMAS TARTLETS

Ingredients
Makes 10–12 ✖✖

Metric/ Imperial		American
225 g/8 oz	flour	2 cups
75 g/3 oz	butter	6 tbsp
4 tbsp	mincemeat	1/3 cup
2	egg whites	2
75 g/3 oz	caster [superfine] sugar	6 tbsp
75 g/3 oz	ground almonds	3/4 cup
15 g/1/2 oz	flaked almonds	2 tbsp
3	glacé cherries	3

Method
Sift the flour into a bowl, add the butter and rub in until the mixture resembles breadcrumbs. Add enough cold water to bind to a dough. Chill for 20 minutes.

Preheat the oven to 190°C/375°F/Gas 5.

Roll out the dough and cut into 7.5-cm/ 3-in rounds. Use to line 10–12 tartlet tins. Divide the mincemeat between the pastry cases.

Beat the egg whites until stiff. Fold in the sugar and ground almonds. Place this macaroon mixture on top of the mincemeat and sprinkle the flaked almonds on top. Quarter the cherries and place one piece in the centre of each tartlet.

Bake for 20 minutes or until golden brown.

IRENE HANDL
•
HAZELNUT CRESCENTS

Ingredients
✖

Metric/ Imperial		American
225 g/8 oz	butter	1 cup
100 g/4 oz	caster [superfine] sugar	1/2 cup
100 g/4 oz	ground hazelnuts	1 cup
225 g/8 oz	flour	2 cups
	vanilla essence [extract]	
	icing [confectioners'] sugar	

Method
Preheat the oven to 200°C/400°F/Gas 6.

Cream the butter with the caster [superfine] sugar until light and fluffy. Add the hazelnuts, flour and a few drops of vanilla essence [extract] and blend well to a smooth dough.

Roll the dough into walnut-size balls, then shape each into a little sausage. Curve the sausages slightly to make half-moons or crescents and arrange on a baking sheet.

Bake for about 15 minutes. Cool slightly on the baking sheet before transferring to a wire rack to cool completely. Dust lightly with icing [confectioners'] sugar, and store in an airtight tin.

Irene Handl

HARRY SECOMBE
•
WELSH CAKES

Ingredients
Makes about 18 ✗

Metric/ Imperial		American
450 g/1 lb	self-raising flour	4 cups
	salt	
225 g/8 oz	butter or margarine	1 cup
100 g/4 oz	sugar	½ cup
225 g/8 oz	currants	1⅓ cups
1	egg	1
300–350 ml/ 10–12 fl oz	milk	1½–1¾ cups
	lard for frying	

Method

Sift the flour and a pinch of salt into a mixing bowl. Cut the butter or margarine into the flour, then rub in until the mixture resembles breadcrumbs. Stir in the sugar and currants. Lightly beat the egg with the milk and add to the dry ingredients. Add only enough milk to bind the ingredients into a soft dough.

Turn the dough onto a floured surface and knead lightly until free from cracks. Roll out the dough to about 5-mm/¼-in thick. Cut into 7.5-cm/3-in rounds.

Rub a griddle with a little lard and place over a moderate heat to warm through. Cook the cakes until brown on the underside, then turn them over and cook for a further 5–7 minutes or until heated through.

Serve hot, with butter.

Harry Secombe

BILLY GRAHAM
•
FRESH APPLE CAKE

Ingredients
✗ ✗

Metric/ Imperial		American
250 ml/8 fl oz	cooking oil	1 cup
450 g/1 lb	sugar	2 cups
2	eggs	2
2 tsp	vanilla essence [extract]	2 tsp
350 g/12 oz	flour	3 cups
½ tsp	salt	½ tsp
1 tsp	bicarbonate of soda [baking soda]	1 tsp
450 g/1 lb	apples	1 lb
100 g/4 oz	chopped nuts	1 cup
Glaze		
150 g/6 oz	brown sugar	1 cup
100 g/4 oz	butter or margarine	½ cup
4 tbsp	evaporated milk	¼ cup
1 tsp	vanilla essence [extract]	1 tsp

Method

Preheat the oven to 150°C/300°F/Gas 2.

Combine the oil, sugar, eggs and vanilla essence [extract] in a mixing bowl and beat well to blend. Sift in the flour, salt and soda and fold together thoroughly. Peel, core and chop the apples. Add to the batter with the nuts. The mixture will be very stiff.

Pour into a long baking pan, about 33 × 23 cm/13 × 9 in. Bake for 1 hour. Allow to cool.

To make the glaze, place the sugar and butter or margarine in a double boiler or in a bowl placed over a pan of boiling water. When melted, add the evaporated milk and bring to the boil. Allow to cool, then stir in the vanilla essence [extract].

Pour the glaze over the cake.

141

INDEX